JIM ZUMBO'S

AMAZING VENISON RECIPES

Happy cooking
Jim Zumbo

BY
JIM ZUMBO

Wapiti Valley Publishing

WAPITI VALLEY PUBLISHING CO.
P.O. Box 2390
Cody, WY 82414
Phone: 307-587-5486
Toll Free: 800-673-4868
Web Site: www.jimzumbo.com

First Printing:	1994
Second Printing:	1995
Third Printing:	1996
Fourth Printing:	1996
Fifth Printing:	1997
Sixth Printing:	1998
Seventh Printing:	1998

ISBN 0-9624025-4-0
Printed in the United States

All photographs in this book by the author.

Amazing Venison Recipes

TABLE OF CONTENTS

FOREWORD

It was bad enough crossing 80 miles of Arctic Ocean waters in a canvas-covered canoe, but when our Inuit guide handed me an unsliced hard-boiled egg between two pieces of bread for lunch, I looked at Zumbo and asked him once again how he managed to talk me into another one of his famous survival hunts.

"Don't worry, Vin," explained Jim. "Our outfitter says we're having raviolis tonight."

For the rest of the day, all I could think of was raviolis. Normal food, at last, I thought. The day before I watched an Inuit boil a duck with head, feathers and innards intact, in a bucket of water. When he believed it was done, he plucked off the feathers and ate the meat. Today, while I ate my egg and bread, I watched our guide eat a raw caribou rib. Yes...I was ready for raviolis.

That night I went into the cook tent for my Italian dinner. There was no place to sit down, so I stood in the corner of the tent. Our outfitter handed me a paper plate and fished a foil packet out of a pot of boiling water. He cut the packet open with his knife and dumped about a dozen of the worst looking raviolis I have ever seen on my paper plate. No sauce! No nothing! Again I looked at Jim with the eyes of a hungry man about to cry.

This was certainly no way to feed a couple of hunters. Jim agreed and I thought our outfitter was in trouble when Zumbo pulled out his knife. But he had other plans.

Jim went out to one of the caribou we had taken the day before. He cut out the two tenderloins. In case you don't know, the tenderloins are two of the most tender pieces of meat on any animal and you find them bordering the backbone on the inside of the chest cavity. When Jim returned with the tenderloins, I knew I was being saved from a night of hunger.

Jim sliced the tenderloins into medallions, coated them heavily with black pepper and a touch of salt and then sautéed the meat until medium rare in butter. It was a quick and easy recipe. The tenderloins tasted great and it was a meal that any hunter could duplicate in every deer camp.

This wasn't the first time I've seen Jim take over the kitchen and the cooking in a hunting camp and in his own home. I've been a guest many times in Jim's home and the Zumbos eat game nearly every day. He keeps two huge freezers full of deer, elk, antelope and whatever other big game animal he gets in his sights. Without a doubt, Jim has cooked more game than any other person I know.

I don't care what anyone says. You can't cook game meat just like any piece of domestic beef. Jim has hunted and cooked all over the world. He has learned how to cook venison and he is a master at it.

Many years ago, I watched Jim broil a tray of bite-sized venison wrapped in bacon. It tasted so good that I now prepare the same tray every Christmas Day. I enjoy cooking and I collect cook books, but I probably have learned more about cooking game from Jim than anyone else.

Why is Jim Zumbo so successful in the kitchen? It's probably because he enjoys cooking nearly as much as hunting. In hunting camps we've shared, Jim is always better than the camp cook. We are indeed fortunate that Jim has decided to share his game cooking secrets with us. But you don't have to believe me. Try some of these big-game recipes and let your palate be your judge.

Good Hunting!

Vin T. Sparano
Editor-In Chief
Outdoor Life

INTRODUCTION

Gamey venison. How many times have you heard that? If you're a hunter, it's probably a household term when discussing it with your friends, spouse, or youngsters. The reason I wrote this book is to share with you my favorite recipes for cooking venison — to make venison really taste great!

Just what is venison? According to most dictionaries, it's the flesh of an ungulate which is a big game species with hooves. Most people define venison as the flesh of deer, but in its correct form, it includes the meat of elk, moose, antelope, caribou, sheep, and other ungulates.

Although the flesh of big game animals varies from species to species, the recipes in this book are basically interchangeable. In other words, a recipe for deer will work for caribou or elk. It's important to note, however, that you should have some idea as to the quality of the venison you're cooking before choosing a recipe. The caribou taken in late August for example will require very little seasoning. That same caribou taken in October may be practically inedible because it was in the rut.

In this book I've selected some of my favorite recipes for the gamiest of all cuts, and I've also described everything you've ever wanted to know about venison — from beginners' tips to gourmet recipes. You'll also see a chapter on busy day recipes which can be used when there's little time to prepare an evening dinner. A chapter on fool proof recipes gives my all time best cures for the very strongest tasting cuts of venison.

This book is the result of a great deal of research throughout my travels, but I'll have to admit that much of that research was pleasant. It's my intention to show you that venison can be enjoyed and savored just as well as the finest cuts of domestic meat. And that it can also easily become a part of your everyday diet that you'll look forward to.

Enjoy!

WHY IS VENISON GAMEY?

You've no doubt read that poor tasting venison is essentially the hunter's fault — that he or she didn't take proper care of the animal in the field. That's the most widespread myth about venison, and I'll touch on some others as well.

How about it — is tough and gamey venison the result of improper field care? To be sure, a carcass that isn't cooled quickly, or isn't immediately field-dressed after being killed, or is hung too long in warm or rainy weather, may indeed be almost inedible by the time it gets to the dinner table. So the answer to the question is a very resounding YES — careless handling will transform an otherwise quality piece of meat into a gamey serving that will require all your culinary skills to make it palatable.

Another chapter details the procedure to properly care for your animal, but my point here is the simple and documented fact that the best care in the world may make no difference in meat quality if the animal fits in any one or more of these categories:

1. It was killed during the peak of the rut (or breeding season).
2. It was very old.
3. It was eating a straight diet of pungent or aromatic plants.
4. It was running extensively before being dispatched.

There are, of course, exceptions to the above. No two animals are alike. Generally speaking, however, meat may be affected if it falls into any of these four categories. Let's examine each of them more closely.

1. A rutting deer often yields poorer quality meat than one taken before the rut. Very few deer are taken AFTER the rut in the U.S. since the seasons are closed by then. However, some southern states have seasons extending into February. Not so in the north, except for some special very late hunts. Deer normally enter the breeding season in mid to late November, running into December, but these periods may vary with the region.

Elk, antelope, moose and caribou, on the other hand, rut earlier, generally in September and October. It's possible to hunt them after the rut is over, as well as before and during the rut.

Pre-rut animals are generally in prime condition, fat and sleek from feeding throughout the summer. That's the time to take the animal at its best, but many hunters have no choice. General elk seasons, for example, usually occur after the rut. Many whitetail seasons begin around the same time as the rut period, and even if they didn't, many hunters prefer hunting whitetails then because the deer are more receptive to rattling and calling. Scrapes and rubs, evident during the whitetail rut, are commonly used by hunters as visual signposts, thus enabling the hunter to pattern deer more effectively.

WHY IS VENISON GAMEY?

These battling whitetail bucks are at the peak of the rut. Many folks believe rutting animals are much stronger tasting than animals taken before or after the rut period.

I recall a fat, juicy whitetail buck I took in the middle of the rut. This deer had lived all its life in and around barley, corn, and oat fields. As soon as it hit the ground, I had it field-dressed; it was hanging within the hour. It was a cool, brisk day; about 30 degrees F. After aging the meat at 35 to 40 degrees for a week, I cut it up, expecting a culinary delight. To my dismay, that buck was as gamey tasting as any I'd ever taken. I concluded that the rut was responsible for its condition, since everything else was going for it. It was young, had fed on grain most of its life, and I dropped it in its tracks as it walked down a wooded trail from feeding in an oat field.

I also recall several very strong-smelling muley bucks I'd taken during the rut. Their flesh was gamey, but those deer also had been feeding on an extensive diet of sagebrush and bitterbrush.

One of the worst tasting animals I'd ever taken was a caribou shot in British Columbia during the peak of the rut. My guide warned me that the meat would be so strong that even the dogs wouldn't eat it. I didn't believe him, but he was right. I had to pull every trick out of the bag to make the meat edible.

I compared that caribou with one I'd taken two months earlier in late August in the Northwest Territories. That bull was outstanding, as delectable as any animal I'd ever eaten. Caribou are often ranked as the very best among all North American big game animals when taken early in the fall. When killed later on during the rut, they're commonly deemed to be practically unfit for human consumption.

WHY IS VENISON GAMEY?

••

Given the fact that venison is affected by the rut, the obvious option is to NOT hunt during the rut. Few of us have that degree of latitude. We hunt when we can, and deal with the meat as best as we can. Then too, hunting during the rut can be much more challenging and/or effective.

2. Shooting a very old animal is something that few hunters accomplish. First off, not many animals get really old in most places where we hunt, especially if there's extensive hunting pressure. In most states, a three year old deer is old. A five-year old deer may be ancient. Secondly, "old" usually translates to big antlers or horns. Trophy-class animals are usually over the hill, as the saying goes. Not many hunters will pass up a big old 12-point whitetail or six-point bull because it might not be good eating. In that case, we're left with venison that may need some extra care and creativity to make it tasty.

In the case of does, or cow elk, it's often difficult to tell their age in the field because there are no antlers to signify how mature they might be. A doe could live 8 to 10 years or older, but the hunter would have no idea of her age. A doe is a doe is a doe. And when a hunter takes a very old doe, she ends up as a surprise on the dinner table — pretty chewy, and probably gamey tasting.

It's no secret that yearling animals are succulent morsels; the very best quality. Not many hunters with an antlerless or either-sex tag however, will purposely shoot a fawn deer or calf elk. If they do, they're in for an epicurean delight.

There are two reasons why hunters shy away from taking yearlings: they're morally opposed, or they figure there's a lot more meat on an adult female. Many whitetail hunters mistake "button bucks" for does when they fill their antlerless or doe tag. Such deer, by the way, are perfectly legal, since it's practically impossible to see the tiny nubbins. A "button buck" is a cute name for a six-month old fawn. I've yet to meet a hunter who can utter the word "fawn" — it seems that it's a tough word to say if you've killed one. Those who do take button bucks will never have better deer meat on the dinner table.

A couple years ago, when Wyoming was being extremely generous with doe/fawn antelope licenses, I had three tags and came home with a doe and two fawns. As to taking the fawns, there was a huge antelope population, and history always repeats itself. If hunters didn't take the surplus, you could lay money that a severe winter would be a grim reaper. Those fawns were so good they could have been passed off as veal to dinner guests, and no one would have been wiser.

3. Some animals, particularly mule deer and antelope, will feed extensively on aromatic plants such as sagebrush, bitterbrush, and other similar shrubs. In some areas, whitetails might also feed on pungent foods.

WHY IS VENISON GAMEY?

◆◆◆

Some people believe that the animals' flesh picks up the strong scent of the plants, and the venison is gamey tasting. As far as I'm concerned, school's out on this one. I'm not convinced either way, though some of my muleys and antelope have been strong tasting long before the rut. These weren't necessarily old animals, either. I have no idea how to confirm this theory. Researchers would have to confine test animals in an enclosure, feed them diets of certain shrubs, and give the animals the taste test. The animals would have to be compared with other deer eating more bland foods in order for the survey to be credible. To my knowledge, this type of testing hasn't been done.

4. Some people believe that an animal that's been running hard before being killed will be tough and gamey tasting. I've had some old-time skilled hunters tell me this. Once again, I don't know of any extensive testing, though a leading researcher tells me that the pH of the meat changes radically in a running animal, thus the aging time must be shortened. He claims there are no other noticeable effects.

If it was true that a running animal tastes bad, then we'd need to take a closer look at deer driving, and hunting deer with hounds (legal in a few southern states). Then too, wounded deer or those that run a distance before expiring would also have a gamier taste. I haven't really noticed any differences in animals that were run hard than those that dropped at the shot, and I'm not sure that we can definitely point the finger at these aspects of hunting and say they're responsible for poorer quality meat.

There's yet one more factor that contributes to the animal's taste: the species itself. An antelope doesn't taste like an elk or a moose; a caribou has it's own subtle taste, etc. Each animal is an individual, affected by its state of health, vigor, age, rut, and other factors. When we shoot an animal, what we have is a wild creature that has its own peculiar taste. My purpose in this book is to be able to eat everything we bring home, from the very best to the very worst, whether we (or someone else) cared for it properly, or it had its own inherent negative qualities. Remember, too, that sometimes we're recipients of meat given to us by other hunters. That meat might have been poorly cared for — we may have no way of knowing. Or maybe we went on a long trip and our meat stayed in camp too long at temperatures warmer than we'd like, or it was in transit too long and not cooled very well. It's up to us to make do with each piece of meat we cook, and to serve it with pride instead of excuses.

Some "purists" believe that venison must taste like venison, that it must not be overwhelmed by spices. I disagree. Everyone's taste is different. The "pure" venison taste is a turn-off to many people. Making it palatable by properly seasoning it and using specific cooking techniques is simply good cooking. Any experienced chef will tell you that - they do it all the time to "regular food".

PROPER FIELD CARE

Some hunting areas are so remote that getting an animal out may be a major ordeal. Before you hunt, make sure you have a sound plan that will allow you to retrieve your animal from the woods.

PROPER FIELD CARE

••

When it comes to food, we civilized humans are well cared for. Thanks to Big Brother in Washington, everything we buy in a store is government inspected or at least must meet certain health standards, whether it's a dozen oranges, a bag of peanuts, or a can of soup.

Meats, of course, come under the strictest guidelines for various reasons. We can get sick on "bad" meat, because of a host of unfriendly bacteria. Meat is also graded according to its quality, so we are insured of getting the particular cut we're paying for. Obviously, we don't want to pay sirloin prices for a round steak. Of course, the meat we buy in the store is chilled, wrapped in a nice sanitary cellophane covering, and is perfectly safe for human consumption.

Compare that "safe" meat with the flesh of an animal that we must deal with in the great outdoors. When you really think about it, the process of transforming the animal from a whole, warm, creature, fully intact with all its internal organs, to a "safe" and edible assemblage of steaks, roasts, chops, etc., is a major accomplishment.

Unlike the slaughter house, or — to be politically correct — the meat-processing facility (goodness), where the animal is killed in a pen, and within minutes is skinned, dressed, and hung in a cooler, the outdoor stage seldom offers such a quick and tidy procedure.

All sorts of factors may complicate the process of transforming your animal into something you'd want to serve on the dinner table. The air temperature may be very warm, requiring you to quickly cool the carcass, often with a great deal of effort. That necessity may be as easy as driving the animal to a cooler to hang it, or figuring a way to cool it when it's a mile or more back in the boonies, and perhaps heavier than you can possibly haul with the gear and assistance you have available. Other than the air temperature, insects and feathered or furred critters will want to share in your bounty, and you may have quite a job dealing with these uninvited pests. If your quarry is large, such as a very heavy deer, or a moose or elk, it could take a day or two to get it to civilization. Likewise, if it falls in a nasty spot, such as in the bottom of a deep ravine or half-way up a mountain, a multi-day ordeal may be required to transport it out. This dilemma may not be of major significance if the air temperature is cold, but if it's warm - watch out. A contaminated carcass could be the result.

Another consideration is the very basic procedure of field-dressing the animal. What you do in this regard may make or break the quality of the carcass.

It becomes quickly obvious that once we've squeezed the trigger and killed an animal, we have a major responsibility of getting the meat to the table.

Proper Field Care

◆◆

The very first act required when your shot is true is to legally tag the animal. Forgetting this simple act may result in an embarrassing encounter with the law. Failure to tag an animal is a top hunting violation in the woods. Next, you must instantly field-dress your prize. Field-dressing is a polite term which really means that you gut the animal (remove the internal organs).

This book won't give you a step-by-step process to field-dressing. At best, pictures in a book are basic guidelines. It's one matter to look at a book's illustrations while sitting in your den or living room, and quite another to recall them when you're in the woods with a carcass at your feet. The very best way to learn is to accompany an experienced hunter. Carefully watch him dress his deer (or your deer). You'll quickly catch on. If you have no mentor, the next best teaching aid is a video. Many films showing field-dressing techniques are available these days.

If you're really green, be prepared for a rather brutal fact of life when you unzipper your first deer. There will be a great deal of blood, and a large supply of intestines, along with the vital organs, and, of course, a peculiar aroma. I've met only one person who truly became nauseous when exposed for the first time to this rather raw sight. For the most part it's an experience that's accepted by most people. To put your mind at ease, if you're about to get in on your first field-dressing experience, my three daughters passed the test with flying colors, all at ages between 12 and 16. These were regular adolescent girls, squeamish at most thing girls are squeamish over, but nonetheless quite comfortable at watching me dress an animal that I (or they) killed.

With the field-dressing procedure done, take steps to quickly cool the carcass. If the air temperature is cool (35 degrees Fahrenheit or colder), mother nature will take care of chilling the meat. Just be sure the cavity is spread apart so heat can escape.

If you've tagged a moose or elk, you'll need to take special precautions. If you intend to leave the carcass overnight, even if the temperature is cold, you must skin the neck area part way to let heat out. These animals have a very thick layer of fur around the neck which provides superb insulation. I recall an elk hunt where I once allowed a field-dressed bull to remain in the snow overnight when the temperature was 18°F. Upon returning the next morning, I discovered the neck meat to be green and already soured. From then on I've skinned the neck of every large animal I've ever taken. Ideally, cut a slit along the underside of the neck and remove the entire windpipe by severing it at both ends.

If the air temperature is warm, you may have to skin a deer on the spot and hang it in the shade if you must leave it in the woods for more than 8 hours. By warm temperatures I'm referring to 60° to 100°F. Many hunts in the south and the west coast occur during warm months; even in the north, temperatures may be hot during some hunts. Be prepared to transport your

PROPER FIELD CARE
◆◆◆

game out of the woods. This might mean simply driving up to the carcass and loading it, or cutting it in pieces and hauling it out of the backwoods on a horse or on your back. Of course, an elk or moose will require much more effort than a deer.

In most cases, a deer is simply dragged out of the woods. Use common sense if much uphill travel is required. It might be wise to cut the carcass in half or in quarters if it's heavy and cumbersome.

A one-wheeled carrying device will make the transportation job much easier. These can be purchased commercially, or homemade. It's a whole lot easier to roll a heavy object on wheels than to carry it on your back.

Pay attention to insects if the weather is warm. Flies will quickly lay eggs on the carcass, but they can be thwarted by wrapping the meat with several layers of cheesecloth. Some people claim that heavy doses of pepper on the meat will repel flies; I haven't found it to be very effective.

If the carcass must be left overnight, be sure to protect it from marauding critters that might like to share your bounty, particularly coyotes and bears. Both can be foiled by hanging the carcass high in a tree and far out on a springy branch so a bear won't climb up and reach it.

During the field-dressing and transportation process, try to keep the meat as clean as possible. Dirt, leaves, twigs, and the fur of the animal itself will soil the flesh and may not be easy to remove afterward, requiring you to do a lot more trimming.

Once again, always think COOL when transporting your meat. Do whatever is required to keep it chilled, even if a great deal of effort is required. Warm meat means spoiled meat, negating all your efforts, and possibly getting you in trouble with the law. Most states have laws that make the waste of game meat a serious violation.

The reward of your extra efforts will be noted at the dinner table. An extra hour or two in the field may make all the difference in great venison or meat that's barely fit to eat.

FROM FIELD TO FREEZER

Snow and cold weather are ideal environments for hunting, because a big game animal can be quickly cooled. The need to cool a carcass is the most important aspect of properly caring for meat.

Aging

Aging meat is done to make it more tender. This happens when enzymes break down the cellular walls of the meat. A commercial processor will take care of aging your meat. If you do it yourself, you can hang your animal by the head or hind legs; I prefer the hind legs because that's the position I use when skinning the carcass.

Beware of neighborhood pets if you hang a carcass from a tree branch or in a barn or garage that's accessible to small animals. I once had a dog visit my garage in which a juicy mule deer buck was hanging by the antlers. The dog chewed off several pounds of choice meat from the hindquarters. From then on, the garage door was closed, or I hung the carcass a couple feet higher if I needed the ventilation.

Proper aging requires the carcass to hang for anywhere from two days to a week or more at ideal temperatures of 35 to 40 degrees with a humidity of around 50 percent. Of course, controlling temperature and humidity reliably is possible only in a refrigerated room. You'll be taking your chances anywhere else.

FROM FIELD TO FREEZER

●●●

You don't absolutely have to age the meat; in some cases it's impossible. Several of my deer were frozen hard as a rock within hours after they were dressed since I took them in temperatures of O degrees or lower. In those cases, my only option, as that of tens of thousands of hunters who hunt in very cold temperatures, is to thaw the carcass in a heated garage, barn, or basement, cut up the meat, and refreeze it. You may have heard horror stories about refreezing meat — don't believe them. A bit of quality may be lost, but you probably won't notice it.

Skinning

Skinning the carcass depends on its size, your initial treatment of the carcass when you prepared to get it out of the woods, and the weather and air temperature. I try to leave the skin on while the carcass is aging and then peel the skin just before I cut up the meat. If a skinned animal is hung more than a day or so, the surface will dry, and you'll have to cut away the hardened outer layering and lose it. The dried crust gets thicker as time passes.

Warm weather requires you to skin the animal immediately, but in cooler weather try to leave the skin on as long as possible.

Using A Commercial Processor

Most big game hunters will take their animal to a commercial meat cutter for processing. Many folks don't have a clue how to cut up a carcass, some don't have the time, and some don't have a place to do it.

If you decide to have it done commercially, beware of the meat cutter who operates in his garage or basement. Some have spotless work areas and keep the meat properly chilled; others have a bad environment in which they work in. The latter translates to poor quality meat — by his careless handling your quality venison could be unfit to eat by the time it gets to your kitchen.

A good meat cutter will work in a clean room, and will have proper tools and machinery. Some small operators don't have a meat grinder. If you want burger ground from your animal — and most people do — ask in advance if the processor will grind meat.

Bear in mind that a processor makes his money on volume — as most business people do. The faster he cuts up a carcass, the more work he can get done in a day. The quickest way to cut up a carcass is to carve out as many roasts as possible. Roasts are big chunks of meat that might otherwise

FROM FIELD TO FREEZER

◆◆

be cut up into steaks, chops, stew meat or burger, all of which take time. Beware of the meat-cutter who suggests that you have a large number of roasts cut from your animal. If you don't care — no problem. If you aren't fond of roasts (remember that roasts are the most difficult cuts to flavor with spices and seasonings), then be precise and instruct the cutter of your wishes.

Check to see that your meat is double-wrapped when you get it from the processor. This should be made clear in advance, but if for some reason it's not, do yourself a favor and wrap it again, relabeling the package. The meat will keep far better when wrapped twice.

Doing It Yourself

You can save money by cutting up your own meat. Unfortunately, plenty of people think this is a deep, dark science that takes a great deal of skill. Not so. You can cut up a carcass yourself with a bit of instruction that you can learn from videos. Granted, you won't always cut the meat "correctly", but who cares? You'll help out your bank account and have the satisfaction of doing it yourself. Many folks find it enjoyable to cut meat as well.

I've been butchering my own game, from squirrels to moose, for more than 30 years, and I've never had a course in meat cutting. I can't honestly say that I cut up a carcass the same way every time, but I manage to do a pretty good job. All it takes is a bit of common sense and basic knowledge of the major meat cuts.

Meat Cutting Tools And Supplies

For tools you'll want a sharp flexible-bladed knife, such as a fish fillet knife. This is ideal for boning out large chunks. A knife with a shorter, stout blade will help in trimming away fat and other jobs. A knife sharpener is a must, since bones will quickly dull the blade. Cut the meat on a clean surface, and have plenty of containers close by to put the cut-up meat in. If possible, choose a work area that is screened from flies if the temperature is warm.

For containers I use large plastic bowls that clean up easily. One bowl is for stew meat, another for meat that will be cut up for burger, and one for steaks. Sirloins and tenderloins are wrapped as soon as they're cut.

Have a supply of quality clear plastic wrap and paper freezer wrap, as well as tape and a marking pen. I use Sharpies, which can be bought in any office supply store.

FROM FIELD TO FREEZER
••

Containers for waste are also necessary. I use three containers, because I dispose of waste in three ways. Marginal meat is cooked and fed to my dog at a ratio of 20 percent meat scraps to 80 percent dry dog food (according to instructions from my veterinarian). Suet is frozen in small portions and used to feed backyard birds in the winter months. The worst of the scraps as well as the bones are properly disposed of. (I often put the entire skeletal system and unusable meat within sight of a window and watch magpies, chickadees, and jays feed on it in the winter).

About Making Burger

Making burger is as easy as putting meat in a grinder and wrapping it. Since venison is dry, with all its fat trimmed away, it's a good idea to add beef or pork suet, the amount depending on your taste and health preference. I prefer adding 10 percent beef or pork suet to the venison. For example, to each five pounds of venison, add one-half pound of suet. If you want to keep your intake of fat lower, you can decrease the amount; if you like moister burger, increase it to as much as 20 percent suet.

I also add seasonings to my burger, preferring a mix of salt, garlic salt, onion salt, pepper, parsley flakes, basil, and oregano. Besides those flavorings, extra strong venison gets a bit of liquid smoke, chili powder, and Worcestershire sauce.

If you add these seasonings, you're really making a form of sausage. The end product to me, however, simply tastes like a zesty burger minus the gamey taste.

A sample proportion of seasonings to five pounds of meat might go like this (but don't be afraid to experiment on your own):

> 1/2 teaspoon salt
> one teaspoon garlic salt
> one teaspoon onion salt
> one teaspoon pepper
> two teaspoons dried parsley flakes
> one teaspoon sweet basil flakes
> one teaspoon dried oregano

You can use two types of grinders; the hand-powered type that is tedious and takes lots of elbow grease, and the electric type, which comes in a small home version or a large commercial version.

I use a small electric model made by Oster. It requires you to cut your meat in small chunks, but it does a fine job. My procedure is to first grind the meat, then grind the suet (you can buy suet either whole or ground from a

FROM FIELD TO FREEZER

◆◆

supermarket) and then mix the two together in a big bowl along with the seasonings. When everything is thoroughly mixed, grind it once more and wrap it in packages that meet your needs.

Wrapping

Use a good-quality freezer wrap, following instructions on the package as to which side to wrap in. With most brands, each side of the freezer paper is different. Wrap the meat tightly, being sure it's sealed from the air. After taping it, wrap it again with another separate layer of paper. Another option is to wrap the meat initially with a quality-brand plastic wrap, then follow with the paper freezer wrap. Cheap plastic is terrible to deal with, since it sticks to itself, and is generally tough to work with. Spend a few extra cents and get the best plastic freezer wrap you can. Label each package with the identity of the meat inside, the type of cut, and date it was wrapped. For example, "Deer tenderloin steaks, 1994". If you have more than one animal, you might want to identify it further.

Freezing

Put the wrapped meat in the freezer immediately, and place it on the racks loosely so air has as much contact as possible. Once the meat is solidly frozen, you can stack the packages tightly together. With upright freezers, packages have a tendency to slide out, and a large area near the door won't be utilized because the packages won't stack. Solve this by using a cardboard box that fits in the space securely; stack the box full of meat. This way you can use every square inch of the freezer. The box should be marked with its contents.

Another wives tale is the life of meat in the freezer. You've probably heard that one year is maximum; I've frozen game meat for up to three years and found it quite satisfactory. I believe that proper wrapping is the key, but you obviously need a quality piece of meat to start with.

FROM FIELD TO FREEZER

MAKING BURGER, WRAPPING, AND FREEZING

Step 1. Cut & trim all fat and thick sinew.

Step 2. Grind meat *(grinder shown here is Oster electric grinder, retails for less than $100).*

Step 3. Basic Ingredients.

Step 4. **Mix ground meat, suet, and spices.**

FROM FIELD TO FREEZER

◆◆

MAKING BURGER, WRAPPING, AND FREEZING

Step 5. Wrap meat in plastic wrap.

Step 6. Wrap meat again in freezer wrap.

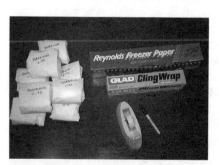

Use quality wrapping material, and be sure to label each package with type of meat and date.

Well stocked freezer. Note cardboard boxes hold meat so it doesn't slide off shelf.

TIPS FOR BEGINNERS

◆◆

If you're a novice at cooking venison, this chapter will detail some very basic rules. Because venison varies a great deal from domestic meats, it must often be prepared and cooked differently. Unfortunately, some people never seem to understand that fact, and go through life slapping venison steaks into a hot frying pan, adding a little salt and pepper, and tolerating the resulting meat, which can be simply awful. They figure that's the way it must be. Of course, some quality cuts of venison can indeed be simply fried with a minimum of spices, but don't count on it. Be prepared for the worst if the meat is in question.

First, do two very important things to all meat. Carefully inspect each piece for hair (fur from the animal's pelt), and remove every wisp you find. Hair will impart a bitter taste to the meat. Second, while you're scrutinizing the venison, trim away every trace of fat. Don't be misled into believing that venison fat is like beef fat. Though beef fat adds moisture and juiciness to the cut, venison fat adds a strong and unnecessary taste.

You'll also notice a silver-colored membrane running through most cuts. This is called silverskin, and though it doesn't contribute negatively to the taste, it's usually tough. Trim it away, even though it means sometimes cutting a steak in two portions since the silverskin may run through the entire steak.

When frying venison steaks, keep the heat on low to medium, because the lack of fat often causes them to burn quickly. The degree of doneness depends on the taste of each person. Don't be intimidated by some so-called venison experts who claim that meat must be done medium rare in order to be "properly" cooked. If you like it well-done, have at it. Cremate it if you like. For best results, trial and error will prove to be your guide. Most people I know like their venison with a tinge of pink in the middle.

I always flour my steaks before I fry them, simply because the taste is always superior to unfloured meat. An easy way to flour meat is to add a quantity of flour to a Zip-lok bag, drop in the meat, seal the bag, and shake it vigorously until all the steaks are coated. When adding spices, put them in the bag of flour and mix it all together, otherwise spices won't stick to meat once it's coated with flour.

If your diet will allow it, a 50-50 mix of olive oil and butter is a superb medium to fry venison in. Otherwise, use a non-cholesterol vegetable oil.

Barbecuing venison is always a challenge because the meat is so dry. Regardless of your care, the steaks will have a tendency to burn or dry out because of the lack of moisture. To solve the problem, baste the steaks every few minutes with a marinade mix, or at least some vegetable oil. Cook the meat slowly, and don't let it overcook on the grill.

TIPS FOR BEGINNERS

◆◆◆

When using venison in stews, cut the meat in chunks no more than one inch square. If the meat is exceptionally gamey, marinate it with one of the mixtures suggested in this book, and refrigerate according to the recipe.

Before putting meat in the stew pot, coat it with flour and brown it in oil. Add the meat to the stew liquid along with sliced onions and celery, the amounts depending on the recipe your using.

I've made stews probably a hundred different ways, and I always start out with browned meat chunks and onion and celery, and then adding the other ingredients as the stew continues to cook. I prefer using a crock-pot to cook stew because it can be left unattended for several hours, and the contents will merrily cook away without burning.

When cooking deerburger that I haven't ground and spiced myself, I put the meat in a large bowl and mix in appropriate spices according to the recipe being followed. By doing so, the flavorings are mixed thoroughly with the meat. Don't be afraid to use your bare hands to mix the meat, after of course you've washed them well.

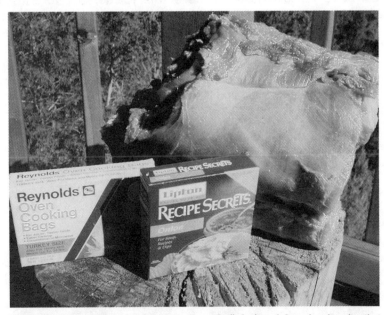

This book offers a number of recipes that are practically foolproof. One of my favorites that any beginner can master quickly is the cooking bag procedure. Simply put a roast in a cooking bag, sprinkle a package of dry onion soup mix on it, and cook for 8 to 10 hours at very low heat — about 200° F. This photo shows an elk neck about to be roasted, but any chunk of venison will do nicely.

A roast is the most unforgiving piece of meat you'll cook because the gamey taste stays locked inside. If you are not fond of real venison flavor,

Tips For Beginners

◆◆

stay away from roasts completely. You can, of course, pierce holes in the meat and push chunks of garlic deep inside, but that doesn't improve the situation all that much. Marinating the roast for a long period of time doesn't really allow the marinade flavor to penetrate. For some reason, a roast seems to improve in flavor the day after it's cooked. I like to shred it and put it in sandwiches loaded with other goodies. More on roasts in the roast chapter.

A lot is said about marinades; in fact I use them a great deal and have included a specific chapter on them. They aren't foolproof, however. Some meat might be so gamey that even a stiff marinade won't neutralize it. Be aware of that possibility.

Gravies will do a great deal to help fend off strong tastes. Don't let gravy-making scare you. If you don't want to make it with drippings from a pan, you can make it from scratch, following easy directions on the package.

Don't be dismayed if the people you're cooking for aren't overly enthusiastic about second helpings. As I've said elsewhere in this book, venison has a distinctive taste. No matter what you do, some folks may not care for it simply because it was venison.

If you try to fool your guests and serve venison but tell them it's beef, be prepared for a fallout if they find out about your trickery. We've all heard the old jokes about cooks making a big stew of various critters — all the guests loved it until they found out what was really in it. Then the dinner wasn't all that great after all, and the cook had to run for his life.

FOOLPROOF RECIPES

◆◆◆

Regardless of the care you take of your venison you will no doubt one day be faced with an exceptionally strong piece of meat. This can happen for reasons already thoroughly discussed in this book.

The following recipes will work on any edible cut of meat regardless of its gamey taste. I've used these recipes over and over and have fine-tuned them to the point where they are practically guaranteed. I'll bet you agree when you try them.

As a tip, soak your gamey meat in milk for at least one hour before cooking. Keep refrigerated while soaking. You'll be amazed at how the milk will neutralize much of the gamey taste. (Whole milk or two-percent milk will work equally well.)

Some recipes have such pungent flavorings that they'll neutralize the nastiest cuts of meat in your freezer. This is the author's favorite, called Ginger Elk (see page 20) but it actually works just as well on deer, antelope, and other animals. Truly an amazing recipe.

Recipes

FOOLPROOF RECIPES

◆◆

GINGER ELK

2 pounds elk steak
5-6 slices ginger root, peeled and cut in 1/4 inch thick slices
1/3 cup ginger root, peeled and minced
2 medium onions, sliced
2 cloves garlic, minced
1 teaspoon sugar
3/4 cup soy sauce
2 to 3 tablespoons vegetable oil
2 tablespoons cornstarch

Cut elk steaks, across the grain, into 1/4 inch thick slices. Layer venison, sliced onions, garlic, and 1/3 cup ginger root in glass bowl. Combine soy sauce and sugar and pour liquid over meat. Cover and refrigerate 45 minutes to one hour.

Heat oil and cook 5 to 6 slices of ginger root until browned and flavor is released into the oil. Remove and discard these ginger slices. Drain the majority of soy sauce from the meat and onion marinade. Add meat, onions, garlic and ginger slices to oil in skillet. Sauté two to three minutes, then sprinkle cornstarch over meat and stir. Continue cooking until meat is completely cooked. Add additional soy sauce to taste. Serves 6.

Notes: Taste the soy sauce. Brands vary, and if the soy sauce is very salty, reduce the marinating time to 30 minutes.

This is Jim Zumbo's favorite all time recipe. Use it for all big game, especially the strongest cuts of meat.

FOOLPROOF RECIPES

••

NO FAIL STEW

3 pounds venison, cut in one-inch chunks
2 quarts water
2 yellow onions, diced
1/2 teaspoon salt
1/2 teaspoon garlic salt
1 teaspoon black pepper
1 large can tomato sauce
4 celery sticks, diced
1/2 head cabbage, chopped
3 tomatoes, chopped
1 tablespoon soy sauce
1 dash liquid smoke
1 dash taco sauce
1/2 cup dry red wine (optional)
1 package chicken gravy mix
1 package brown gravy mix
1 package Au Jus mix
1 can corn
1 green pepper, diced
3 potatoes, diced
3 carrots, diced

Place venison, water, onion, salt, garlic salt, pepper, tomato sauce, celery, and cabbage in pan or slow cooker, and cook 2-1/2 to 3 hours. Add tomatoes, soy sauce, liquid smoke, taco sauce, wine, all package mixes, corn, green pepper, and cook another 45 minutes. Add potatoes and carrots and cook an additional 20 to 30 minutes until potatoes are tender.
Serves 6-8.

FOOLPROOF RECIPES

UNREAL STEW FOR GAMEY MEAT

2 pounds meat, cut in 1-inch squares
1/2 pound bacon
2 quarts water
1 large onion, diced
5 stalks celery and leaves, diced
3 bay leaves
1/2 teaspoon salt
1/2 teaspoon garlic salt
1/2 teaspoon pepper
1 teaspoon parsley
1 yellow pepper, chopped
1 red pepper, chopped
12 dashes teriyaki sauce
2 tablespoons A-1 sauce
1 package brown gravy mix
1 package chicken gravy mix
1 package chili mix
6 fresh mushrooms, diced
1 large can tomato juice
4 medium tomatoes, diced
4 potatoes, diced
4 carrots, diced

Brown bacon and set aside. Brown meat in bacon grease until it loses its pink color. Place meat and bacon in pot (or slow cooker) and cover with 2 inches of water. Add onion, celery, bay leaves, salt, garlic salt, pepper, and parsley to pot. Cook 2 or more hours until meat is tender adding water as necessary. After meat is tender, add yellow and red pepper, teriyaki and A-1 sauce, gravy mixes, chili mix, mushrooms, and tomato juice and cook for 30 minutes. Add diced tomatoes, potatoes, carrots and cook until vegetables are tender.

Note: this stew is great for any tough, gamey meat!

FOOLPROOF RECIPES

◆◆◆

WESTERN CHILI

2 pounds ground venison
1/4 cup cooking oil
1 cup chopped onion
2 cloves garlic, minced
1 large green pepper, chopped
3 tablespoons chili powder
2 cups whole tomatoes
1 cup tomato sauce
1 cup water
1/2 teaspoon salt
1 tablespoon flour mixed with 2 tablespoons water
3 cups cooked kidney beans

Brown ground venison in oil in a Dutch oven until meat loses its pink color. Add onion, garlic and green pepper. Cook for 5 minutes longer. Add chili powder, tomatoes, tomato sauce, water and salt. Simmer for 2 hours. Add the flour paste and cook until mixture thickens. Add the kidney beans and cook another 15 minutes. Serve hot with French bread or hot biscuits. Serves 6 to 8.

FOOLPROOF RECIPES

◆◆

STIR-FRY VENISON

2 pounds venison round steak
1/4 cup oil
2 small onions, sliced
6 large mushrooms, sliced
2 stalks celery, chopped
1 green pepper, chopped
1/2 cup chicken broth
1/4 teaspoon dry mustard
1 teaspoon cornstarch mixed with 2 tablespoons water

Cut meat, against the grain, into strips about 1/4 inch thick and marinate as shown below. Cut vegetables immediately before cooking. Heat 1/4 cup oil in wok, add meat and stir-fry for 2 minutes. Push to the side, add the onions, and stir-fry 2 minutes longer. Again, push to the side, and add mushrooms, stir-fry for 2 additional minutes. Add celery and fry for 2 minutes; then green pepper and fry for 1 minute. Gradually add chicken broth and dry mustard to mixture in wok, when broth begins to bubble add cornstarch mixture, stirring constantly until it thickens. Serve over rice. Serves 6 to 8.

Marinade

1 cup cooking oil
1/3 cup soy sauce
1/4 teaspoon ground ginger
1/8 teaspoon cayenne pepper

Combine ingredients in a glass bowl. Add meat and marinate in refrigerator for 3 hours.

FOOLPROOF RECIPES

••

STEAK & BROCCOLI CURRY

1 1/2 pounds tender venison round steak
2 tablespoons soy sauce
1/2 teaspoon sugar
1 1/2 cups beef broth
3 tablespoons flour
2 teaspoons curry powder
1/2 teaspoon salt
3 tablespoons cooking oil
1 medium onion, cut into wedges
3 cups fresh broccoli buds, cut into 1-inch pieces
Chow mein noodles

Slice steak into thin strips across the grain. Place in bowl and sprinkle with soy sauce and sugar. Set aside. Stir together broth, flour, curry powder and salt. Set aside. Heat wok or large skillet over high heat. Add 2 tablespoons of cooking oil. Stir-fry onion wedges and broccoli for 4 minutes. Remove vegetables. Add remaining oil to wok and stir-fry half of the meat for 3 minutes and push to side of wok. Repeat with remainder of meat. Stir flour-broth mixture and add to center of wok. Cook and stir until bubbly. Return vegetables to wok, stir, cover and cook 3 minutes more. Serve over chow mein noodles.

FOOLPROOF RECIPES

◆◆

VENISON & BACON

3 pounds venison, cubed
3 tablespoons olive oil
3 onions, chopped
3 garlic cloves, minced
1/2 pound bacon, diced
1 teaspoon curry powder
1 1/2 quarts water
2 teaspoons bourbon whiskey (optional)
1/4 cup beer
1 teaspoon salt
1/2 pound fresh mushrooms, sliced

Brown meat in olive oil in a Dutch oven. Add onions, garlic and bacon. Cook until onions are soft and shiny, stirring frequently. Add remaining ingredients except for mushrooms; cover and simmer for 1 1/2 hours or until meat is tender. Add mushrooms and simmer 20 minutes more. Serve over rice. Serves 8 to 10.

FOOLPROOF RECIPES

◆◆◆

JIM'S POT-LUCK CASSEROLE

2 pounds ground venison
2 tablespoons cooking oil
1/4 teaspoon garlic salt
1/2 teaspoon onion salt
10 3/4-ounce can condensed chicken noodle soup
10 3/4-ounce can condensed tomato soup
1/2 teaspoon chili powder
1/4 cup bottled taco sauce
1/2 teaspoon parsley flakes
6 slices Monterey jack cheese, (1" x 3" x 1/4")

In a large, heavy skillet, brown venison in oil, seasoning with garlic salt and onion salt as it cooks. When meat has lost all pink color, add the remaining ingredients except for the cheese. Mix lightly and transfer into a large casserole. Place cheese on top of mixture and bake for 30 minutes at 350°F or until the meat mixture is hot and the cheese is melted. Serve on toast or rice. Serves 6.

MARINADES

◆◆◆

Marinades are used to flavor and/or tenderize tough and gamey meat. The sky's the limit when it comes to marinade ingredients. The basics include an acid, an oil, and flavorings. This chapter details some outstanding marinades, but don't be afraid to experiment yourself.

A marinade is nothing more than a mixture that will tenderize and/or alter the taste of your venison. A standard marinade has three basic ingredients: an oil, an acid, and flavorings. There are literally thousands of marinade possibilities but practically all of them have these three components. Generally speaking, the acid breaks the meat down — making the cut more tender, the oil keeps the meat from drying out, and the flavorings change or neutralize the taste of the meat.

Oils can consist of olive, safflower, canola, corn, peanut, or others. Acids are usually vinegar such as plain distilled white, cider or wine vinegar, and can also include citrus juices from lemons and limes, or wines, and other acidic juices such as soy sauce. Seasonings vary a great deal but often include garlic, onion, and a variety of herbs.

Because of the acidic nature of marinades, it's necessary to put them in a glass or plastic container and keep the dish under refrigeration, turning the meat frequently during the marinating period. As a tip, place your meat and marinade liquid in a Zip-lock type bag and seal tightly. You can then simply shake the bag and turn it over when it's time to mix the contents.

Some of these marinades are detailed in specific recipes throughout the book, but I feel they are good enough to be interchangeable and can be used in other recipes. Or, be creative and use them for your own special dishes.

MARINADES

•••

Recipes

SUE'S MARINADE

1/3 cup white wine
1/3 cup soy sauce
3 tablespoons vegetable oil
2 cloves garlic, minced
1 teaspoon vinegar
1-1/2 teaspoons brown sugar
1/2 teaspoon ground ginger

Shake all above ingredients in jar and pour over meat. Marinate at least 3 to 3-1/2 hours, or overnight. If left overnight, refrigerate and stir occasionally. Recipe is enough for 2 to 3 pounds of venison steak.

This recipe compliments of Sue Gooding, Albuquerque, New Mexico

Marinades

◆◆◆

Charlie's Marinade

> 1 cup lemon juice (fresh squeezed or bottled)
> 1/2 cup soy sauce
> 1 cup white vinegar
> 1/2 cup bourbon or scotch (optional)
> 3 tablespoons black pepper, finely ground
> 3 tablespoons cayenne pepper, finely ground
> 4 tablespoons brown sugar
> 3 tablespoons Habanero pepper sauce*

Combine all ingredients and mix well. Marinate meat overnight in refrigerator using about one cup per one pound of meat. If a thicker marinade is desired, add one cup of catsup.

* Note: If you are unable to obtain Habanero Pepper Sauce, substitute 2 cloves of crushed garlic for each cup of marinade.

This recipe compliments of Charlie McLeod, Fallston, Maryland

Marinade #1

> 2 cloves garlic
> 1 teaspoon coriander
> 3 tablespoons diced yellow onion
> 1 tablespoon brown sugar
> 2 tablespoons light soy sauce
> dash of Tabasco
> 2 tablespoons lemon juice
> 3 tablespoons dry sherry
> 1 to 1-1/2 pounds venison round steak

Combine above marinade ingredients in glass bowl and mix well. Cut up round steak by slicing it into thin ropes about 3/8 inch thick. Place meat in Marinade and refrigerate for at least one hour.

See also: Skewered Steak With Peanut Sauce recipe.

MARINADES

••

MARINADE #2

1/2 cup vinegar
2 cups water
Juice from one lemon
1/2 cup olive oil

Combine above ingredients in glass bowl and marinate roast overnight.

See also: Green Creek Roast recipe.

MARINADE #3

1 small onion, chopped
2 teaspoons thyme
1 bay leaf
1 cup wine vinegar
1/2 cup cooking oil
2 teaspoons melted butter
1 tablespoon lemon juice

Combine above ingredients in glass bowl. Add meat and mix well. Cover and refrigerate 8 hours or overnight.

See also: Pepper Steak recipe.

MARINADES

●●

MARINADE #4

1 medium onion, sliced
2 bay leaves
1/2 teaspoon leaf oregano
1/4 teaspoon pepper
1/2 teaspoon salt
4 cups red wine
2 tablespoons olive oil

Combine above ingredients in glass bowl. Add meat and mix well. Cover and refrigerate for 3 hours, turning frequently.

See also: Venison Pot Roast recipe.

MARINADE #5

1 medium onion, sliced
2 cloves garlic, peeled and halved lengthwise
1 bay leaf
1/2 teaspoon dried rosemary
1/2 teaspoon thyme
1/4 teaspoon dried basil
1/4 teaspoon pepper
4 cups red wine

Prepare marinade by combining above ingredients. Marinate meat for 3 hours, turning frequently.

See also: Venison Pot Roast recipe

MARINADES

••

MARINADE #6

1 cup cooking oil
1/3 cup soy sauce
1/4 teaspoon ground ginger
1/8 teaspoon cayenne pepper

Combine ingredients in a glass bowl. Add meat and marinate in refrigerator for 3 hours.

See also: Stir-Fry Venison recipe.

MARINADE #7

12 ounces beer
1/3 cup diced onion
2 tablespoons cooking oil
3/4 teaspoon salt
1 teaspoon curry powder
1/2 teaspoon ground ginger
1/4 teaspoon garlic powder

In a glass bowl, combine beer, onion, oil, salt, curry powder, ginger and garlic powder. Pour marinade over meat, and refrigerate for 4 to 5 hours.

See also: Venison Kabobs Carbonade recipe.

MARINADES

••

MARINADE #8

1/2 cup tequila
3 tablespoons lime juice
2 tablespoons olive oil
1 teaspoon freshly grated orange peel
1 small dried red pepper, crushed

Trim fat from meat. Rub salt into meat and place in a shallow dish. Combine tequila, lime juice, olive oil, (see recipe noted below) orange peel and pepper. Pour over meat and refrigerate 6 to 8 hours, turning every few hours.

See also: South Of The Border recipe.

MARINADE #9

12 ounces beer
1 cup Italian oil-and-vinegar salad dressing

Combine beer and salad dressing for marinade. Marinate in refrigerator overnight. Enough for 2 pounds of meat.

See also: Hobo Fajitas recipe.

APPETIZERS & SNACKS

◆◆

This Venison Bean Salad is a refreshing treat that prepares the palate for the main dish to come. (See page 44)

Recipes

APPETIZERS & SNACKS

••

BUTTERED VENISON

2 pounds venison steaks or strips
1/2 teaspoon garlic salt
3 tablespoons cooking oil

Cut meat into very thin strips, rub with oil, and sprinkle with salt. Broil, turning frequently to sear meat. Continue cooking until the desired state of doneness is achieved. Spread butter paste on each slice. Serve immediately. Serves 6.

Butter Paste

1/4 cup soft butter
1/2 teaspoon salt
1/2 teaspoon onion salt
1/2 teaspoon pepper
1 tablespoon chopped parsley
1 1/2 tablespoons lemon juice

Blend salts, pepper and parsley into butter. Add lemon juice and beat until smooth.

Appetizers & Snacks

◆◆

Simply Simple Venison Strips

1 1/2 pounds venison steak
Soy Sauce
1 egg
1/2 teaspoon minced onion flakes
Cracker crumbs
1/4 to 1/2 teaspoon salt
1/4 teaspoon garlic salt
1/4 teaspoon pepper

Cut venison into 1" x 3" strips. Douse meat lightly with soy sauce and let sit 10 minutes. Beat egg with onion flakes. Dip meat strips in egg mixture and then in cracker crumbs. Deep fry in hot oil until golden brown. Season with salts and pepper. Makes excellent family snacks or hors d'oeuvres.

Bacon-Elk Wraps

1 pound elk steaks
1/2 pound bacon

Cut meat into one inch squares, and wrap each piece with a strip of bacon about 2-1/2 to 3 inches long. Pierce through the bacon and meat with a toothpick to secure the roll. Skewer 6 to 7 "wraps" onto a bamboo or metal skewer stick and place on a broiler rack. Broil until one side is lightly brown, turn and cook the other side. Serve hot. Makes 24 to 30.

Tip: For gamey meat, marinate the meat chunks in soy sauce for about 30 minutes before cooking.

See next page for easy assembly.

This recipe compliments of Marge Bailey, Cody, Wyoming.

APPETIZERS & SNACKS

◆◆◆

MAKING BACON-ELK WRAPS

A real party pleaser. Guaranteed, there won't be any leftovers!

Step 1. Bacon, meat chunks cut 1"
square, skewers, and toothpicks
ready for assembly.

Step 2. Roll each piece of meat in
a 3" strip of bacon and pierce with
a toothpick.

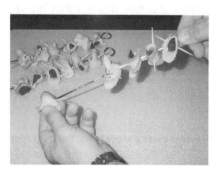

Step 3. Put six to eight pieces on
each skewer.

Step 4. Place meat on broiler pan
and put in oven. Turn pieces until
done to desired bacon crispness.

Step 5. Remove from skewer and
serve.

APPETIZERS & SNACKS

◆◆

VENISON POT STICKERS

  1 pound ground venison
  1 1/2 cups nappa cabbage, chopped
  1/3 cup onion, chopped
  1 1/2 tablespoons chopped fresh ginger root
  1 teaspoon garlic, minced
  1 teaspoon soy sauce
  2 teaspoons sesame seed oil
  1 teaspoon salt
  1 teaspoon wine
  1/2 teaspoon sugar
  2 tablespoons cornstarch
  vegetable oil for frying
  2 1/2 cups chicken broth
  1/2 package of Siu Mai (gyoza) wrappers

Combine all ingredients except frying oil, chicken broth and Siu Mai wrappers. Place 2 teaspoons of the mixture in the center of the Siu Mai wrapper, moisten the edge with water, fold the wrapper in half and press the edges together to form a half-circle. Using a 12 inch skillet, heat enough oil to cover the bottom of the pan. Fry the pot stickers in batches on medium high heat until brown on all sides. When all the pot stickers have been fried, return them to the skillet and pour the soup stock over them. Cover and cook until the soup stock is absorbed. Serve hot with soy sauce for a dip. Yield about 40; makes a great appetizer!

This recipe compliments of Kim Zumbo, Bountiful, Utah.

APPETIZERS & SNACKS

QUICK VENISON CANAPÉS

2 cups cooked slices of venison roast
1/8 cup Bread and Butter pickles
1/8 cup dill pickles
3 tablespoons grated onion
1/2 cup mayonnaise
1 to 2 teaspoons brown spicy prepared mustard
1/2 cup grated cheddar cheese
Salt
Pepper
Garlic salt
Pimento, chopped

Grind leftover meat with pickles and onion in meat grinder. Add enough mayonnaise to make mixture a spreadable consistency. Add mustard and mix well. Add grated cheese and seasonings to taste. Spread on crackers or bread rounds and top with pimento for color. Also, makes a great spread for sandwiches.

APPETIZERS & SNACKS

••

VENISON CRESCENT APPETIZER

2 tablespoons cooking oil
1 pound ground venison
1/2 teaspoon dried minced onion
1/4 teaspoon celery salt
1/4 teaspoon garlic salt
1/4 teaspoon salt
1/8 teaspoon pepper
1/4 teaspoon paprika
1 tablespoon soy sauce
30 unbaked refrigerated crescent rolls

Preheat oven to 400°F. Heat oil in skillet and brown venison with dried seasonings until all the meat is cooked through. Stir in soy sauce. Unroll preshaped crescent dough and roll out into flat triangles. Place 1 to 2 teaspoons of meat mixture in the center of each triangle. Roll up carefully and place on greased baking sheet. Bake for 10 to 15 minutes or until crescents are golden brown.

APPETIZERS & SNACKS

••

CHISLIC

2 pounds venison, cut into 1/2-inch cubes
1 cup cooking oil
1/2 teaspoon salt
1/8 teaspoon pepper
1/4 teaspoon garlic salt
1/4 teaspoon onion salt

Fry meat in deep fat until tender. Sprinkle salt, pepper, garlic and onion salts on meat and serve with Barbecue Sauce and crackers.

JERKY TRAIL SNACK

Jerky
Unsalted, roasted peanuts
Cashews
Raisins
Dates, chopped
Sunflower seeds
M & M candy-coated chocolate candies
Dried bananas

Use your favorite jerky recipe. Cut jerky into small bits and add equal portions of other ingredients. Put a handful or two into your backpack to keep you going in any situation. Use your imagination to create a nutritional, or quick energy snack.

APPETIZERS & SNACKS

••

VENISON SUMMER SALAD

1 1/2 cups cooked venison roast, diced
4 cups romaine lettuce, torn into bite-sized pieces
3 cups fresh spinach, torn into bite-sized pieces
3 fresh medium peaches, peeled, pitted and sliced
1 ripe avocado, peeled, pitted and sliced
12 cherry tomatoes, halved
1/2 cup salad oil
3 tablespoons vinegar
1 teaspoon prepared horseradish
1/2 teaspoon salt
1/2 teaspoon Worcestershire sauce
1/8 teaspoon pepper
2 drops bottled hot pepper sauce
Croutons

In salad bowl, combine cooked venison, romaine, spinach, sliced peaches, sliced avocado and cherry tomato halves. In a small jar combine salad oil, vinegar, horseradish, salt, Worcestershire sauce, pepper and hot pepper sauce. Cover and shake well. Just before serving, pour dressing mixture over salad and toss lightly. Top with croutons. Serves 6 to 8.

Appetizers & Snacks

◆◆◆

Venison Bean Salad

> 1/3 cup mayonnaise
> 1/4 cup chili sauce
> 1 tablespoon sweet pickle relish
> 1/2 teaspoon salt
> 8 ounces canned kidney beans, drained
> 2 cups cooked venison roast, diced
> 1 cup chopped celery
> 1/2 cup chopped onion
> 4 eggs, hard boiled, peeled and chopped

Blend together mayonnaise, chili sauce, sweet pickle relish and salt in a jar. Combine beans, meat, celery, onion and eggs in a mixing bowl. Add mayonnaise mixture to bowl and mix. Cover and refrigerate up to 24 hours. Stir salad just before serving. Serves 4 to 5.

Venison Barbecued Sandwiches

> 2 cups cooked venison steak, cubed
> 12-ounces chili sauce (bottled, or your favorite recipe)
> 8 ounces canned tomato sauce
> 1 sliced onion
> 2 tablespoons chopped green pepper
> 1 tablespoon Worcestershire sauce
> 1 1/2 teaspoons prepared mustard
> 1/4 teaspoon salt
> 1 teaspoon salsa sauce
> 6 hamburger buns

Blend meat in blender until coarsely chopped. Place chopped venison in a saucepan. In blender, combine chili sauce, tomato sauce, onion, green pepper, Worcestershire sauce, mustard, salt and salsa sauce. Cover and blend until vegetables are chopped. Stir into meat; simmer, covered 15 to 20 minutes. Spoon 1/4 cup onto each bun. Serves 6.

STEAKS

●●

Any given animal will produce a wide variety of steaks, from quality cuts, such as the sirloin and the backstrap, to the tougher cuts. For that reason, steaks should be identified as much as possible before being cooked so you know how to treat them.

On the better cuts for example, mechanical or artificial tenderizing with a mallet or a tenderizing marinade probably won't be needed. On the lesser quality cuts however, you should always consider using some form of tenderizing.

I tenderize all my steaks as a matter of course except for the choice cuts. I have a variety of mallets and a Jaccard Tenderizing Machine that has 48 sharp blades and does an excellent job.

When pounding meat, first trim away all the fat and hit it vigorously with the hammer, but not so hard that the hammer goes completely through the steak. Most meat mallets are two sided, one with a coarser edge than the other. Hit the meat with the coarse edge first and then pound on it with the finer edge. Turn the meat over and repeat the process. When you are done, the meat should have been enlarged to at least twice its size or more.

I always like to tenderize my steaks before putting them in a marinade. That way the liquid has access to the freshly pounded meat. Also, if you try to hammer meat that is moist with marinade you are apt to splatter marinade around your kitchen. Not a good idea.

I almost always flour my steaks before I cook them because I believe it adds extra flavor. Before flouring however, I first season the steaks with my spices and then coat them with flour. If you try flouring the meat first, the flour will seal the meat completely and the spices won't adhere to it. I prefer cooking steaks on low to medium heat and consider them done when they are just barely pink. Before they reach that point, I'll often toss in some onions and mushrooms, add a quarter cup of wine and let the whole works simmer for a few minutes before serving.

The following recipes include some that work well with gamey meat. If you're cooking gamey meat, choose those that have marinades as well as stronger herbs and spices.

STEAKS

◆◆◆

One of the major reasons that venison is gamey is improper cooking. Be more creative than simply frying steaks in cooking oil and hoping for the best. This dish, Iowa Venison Delight, (see page 57) will make you a believer in venison.

Recipes

STEAKS

TENDERIZING MEAT

Both the wooden and metal meat mallets work well, as does the Jaccard Tenderizing Machine (top).

Note size of steaks after being processed. Steak on right was tenderized with Jaccard; steak on lower left was pounded with mallet.

To use hammer, pound meat on each side, first using coarse side of hammer, then fine side.

Soaking meat in milk helps tenderize as well as neutralize gamey tastes.

Jaccard tool has 48 sharp blades (shown here) that puncture and tenderize meat.

••

STEAK IN MUSHROOM GRAVY

1-1/2 to 2 pounds steak
flour
salt
pepper
garlic salt
2 cans cream of mushroom soup

Coat cut up steak pieces with flour and brown in hot oil. Season with salt, pepper, and garlic salt. Remove steak pieces to a casserole dish or slow cooker. Cover steaks with soup. Cook in slow cooker or 325°F oven until tender.

This recipe can also be used for cooking grouse, pigeons, doves or other game birds.

OVEN BAKED STEAK

2 to 2-1/2 pounds steak
3/4 cup flour
1 package dry onion soup mix
1/4 cup water

Coat steak with flour. Brown in oil at medium high heat. Remove from fry pan and put in casserole dish that has been sprayed with non-stick spray. Sprinkle dry onion soup mix over browned meat. Pour 1/4 cup water in dish. Cover and bake at 350 degrees for 30 minutes. Remove lid and bake for 15 minutes more uncovered.

These recipes compliments of Bruce & Elaine Koffler, Koffler Boats, Junction City, Oregon

●◆◆

SKEWERED STEAK WITH PEANUT SAUCE

Marinade

> 2 cloves garlic
> 1 teaspoon coriander
> 3 tablespoons diced yellow onion
> 1 tablespoon brown sugar
> 2 tablespoons light soy sauce
> dash of Tabasco
> 2 tablespoons lemon juice
> 3 tablespoons dry sherry
> 1 to 1-1/2 pounds venison round steak

Combine above marinade ingredients in glass bowl and mix well. Cut up round steak by slicing it into thin ropes about 3/8 inch thick. Place meat in Marinade and refrigerate for at least one hour.

Remove meat from marinade and skewer in 'S' shape patterns on bamboo or stainless steel skewers. Place on broiler pan and broil 4 to 5 inches from source of heat. Turn skewers when top side is well browned. Top with Peanut Sauce and serve immediately.

Peanut Sauce

> 1/2 cup yellow onion, diced
> 2 tablespoons of brown sugar
> 1 tablespoon lemon juice
> 1 cup dry roasted peanuts, chopped
>
> 1/4 cup butter
> 1/2 cup soy sauce
> Dash of Tabasco

Sauté diced yellow onion in butter. Add remaining ingredients and warm throughout.

STEAKS

◆◆

CHICKEN FRIED VENISON

2 pounds (4 pieces) venison steak
1 beaten egg
1/4 teaspoon garlic salt
1/4 teaspoon onion salt
1/2 cup flour
Salt
Pepper
Cooking oil

Trim all fat from steaks and cut any visible membrane in meat to prevent curling during frying. Tenderize and dip each piece in egg, then in a mixture of garlic salt, onion salt and flour. Sprinkle with salt and pepper to taste and fry in cooking oil until done. Serves 4.

SOUPED-UP STEAKS

2 pounds venison steak (4 to 5 pieces)
10 3/4 ounces condensed cream of mushroom soup
10 3/4 ounces condensed cream of chicken soup
1/2 cup dry red wine
1/2 teaspoon onion salt
1/4 teaspoon white pepper
1/2 cup canned mushrooms

Mix all ingredients except for the meat together in a casserole dish. Place steaks in mixture, turning to coat all portions of meat, making sure soup mixture covers meat. Add a little water if necessary. Cover and bake at 350°F for 1 1/2 hours. Serves 4 to 5.

STEAKS

••

BETTY'S VENISON CHOPS

1/4 teaspoon onion salt
1/2 teaspoon salt
1/4 teaspoon pepper
3 tablespoons flour
4 venison chops or steaks (1 1/2 to 2 pounds)
4 tablespoons oil
1/2 cup ketchup
1/2 cup vinegar
1/2 teaspoon garlic salt
1 teaspoon liquid smoke
1 tablespoon Worcestershire sauce
Dash Tabasco sauce

In a small shallow bowl, mix together onion salt, salt, pepper and flour. Dip chops or steaks in mixture and coat on all sides. Fry meat in oil until brown. Mix remaining ingredients in a small bowl. Pour over browned meat and simmer until meat is tender for 1 1/2 hours. Serves 4.

◆◆◆

British-Style Chops

2 pounds venison chops
Salt
Pepper
2 tablespoons butter
3 tablespoons warmed gin
2 crushed juniper berries
1/4 teaspoon leaf basil
1/2 cup warmed heavy cream
Juice of 1/4 lemon

First make Brown Sauce recipe given below. Sprinkle meat with salt and pepper. In a skillet, brown chops in butter, cooking about 5 minutes on each side. Place chops in shallow baking dish away from heat. Add gin to the skillet and ignite. When the flames die, stir and scrape the pan to get everything into the liquid. Add juniper berries, basil and brown sauce, stirring over low heat. Slowly add cream and blend. When the mixture is heated through, add lemon juice and then pour liquid mixture over chops. If necessary, reheat the chops in a 350°F oven until warm, but don't let the sauce come to a boil. Serves 4.

Brown Sauce

2 tablespoons margarine
2 tablespoons flour
2 1/4 cups beef consommé or bouillon
Salt and Pepper to taste

In a skillet melt butter and blend in flour, cooking and stirring over low heat until mixture is light brown. Gradually add consommé or bouillon, stirring until smooth. Bring to a boil and stir rapidly for 3 to 4 minutes. Lower heat and simmer for 20 minutes, stirring often to prevent sticking. Remove from heat and season with salt and pepper to taste.

STEAKS

◆◆◆

HUNGARIAN VENISON BAKE

2 pounds venison steak
1/2 cup flour
1 tablespoon paprika
1/2 teaspoon salt
1/4 teaspoon pepper
4 tablespoons oil
1/2 cup canned mushrooms
1 beef bouillon cube
1 cup canned whole tomatoes
1/4 cup chopped green pepper
2 stalks celery, finely diced
1/2 cup dry red wine

Pound meat with a meat mallet and cut into bite-sized pieces. Combine flour, paprika, salt and pepper. Dredge meat in mixture and brown in hot oil. Remove to a baking dish. Drain liquid from mushrooms. Add enough water to mushroom liquid to make one cup. Heat mushroom liquid and water until it comes to a boil. Dissolve bouillon cube in mushroom liquid and pour over meat. Bake at 350°F for 45 minutes. Combine tomatoes, green pepper, mushrooms, celery and wine. Remove meat from oven and pour tomato mixture into dish. Bake 15 to 20 minutes longer. Serves 6 to 8.

••

STEAK & MUSHROOM ROLL-UP

2 pounds venison round steak, 1/2 inch thick
1/2 pound fresh mushrooms, sliced
1 small onion, diced
1/4 cup celery, diced
3 tablespoons butter or margarine
1 cup dry breadcrumbs
1 tablespoon Worcestershire sauce
1 tablespoon parsley
1 teaspoon basil
Salt
Pepper
Garlic salt
2 to 4 tablespoons cooking oil
1 cup dry red wine

Trim steak into a square shape. Sauté celery, onions and mushrooms in butter. In a bowl, combine sautéed mushroom mixture with breadcrumbs, Worcestershire sauce, parsley and basil. Sprinkle steak with salt, pepper, and garlic salt. Spread mushroom mixture onto meat and roll up loosely like a jelly roll. Tie in 3 or 4 places with string. Sear on all exposed sides in a Dutch oven in cooking oil. Pour in wine and bake uncovered in a 325°F oven for about 2 to 2 1/2 hours or until tender. Serves 6.

•••

BREADED VENISON CUTLETS

1 beaten egg
1/2 teaspoon salt
1/8 teaspoon pepper
1 pound venison round steak, 1/4 inch thick
3/4 cup dry breadcrumbs
1/2 teaspoon parsley
1/2 teaspoon sweet basil
1/8 teaspoon oregano
1/4 cup margarine

Beat egg, salt and pepper with a fork. Combine breadcrumbs with herbs. Dip meat in egg mixture and then coat well with breadcrumb mixture. Let cutlets sit for 5 minutes. Then fry meat in margarine for 1 to 2 minutes on each side until golden brown and meat loses pink color. Serve immediately. Serves 6 to 8.

DEVILED VENISON ROULADE

1 1/2 pounds venison steak
4 tablespoons hot water
3 tablespoons dry onion soup mix
3 tablespoons horseradish mustard
Salt
Pepper
4 ounces canned mushrooms, sliced
2 tablespoons butter or margarine

Preheat broiler. Cut venison into 4 thin steaks and score each piece with a knife. Mix water and dry soup and let stand 5 minutes. Stir in horseradish mustard. Sprinkle steaks with salt and pepper. Spread each steak with a fourth of the mustard mixture and top each with a fourth of the mushrooms. Roll up and fasten with toothpicks. Brush with melted butter. Broil until meat loses pink color throughout, turning and basting frequently with more butter. Serves 4.

STEAKS

••

PEPPER STEAK

Marinade

1 small onion, chopped
2 teaspoons thyme
1 bay leaf
1 cup wine vinegar
1/2 cup cooking oil
2 teaspoons melted butter
1 tablespoon lemon juice

Combine ingredients in glass bowl. Add meat and mix well. Cover and refrigerate 8 hours or overnight.

2 pounds venison round steak (cut 2 inches thick)
2 teaspoons unseasoned meat tenderizer
1/2 cup whole peppercorns, coarsely ground

Marinate meat as shown above. When ready to cook, drain off marinade and reserve juices for basting. Pound pepper and tenderizer into meat. Grill over hot coals, basting periodically with marinade until meat is well done. Cut meat into 1/2 inch strips and serve. Serves 6 to 8.

STEAKS

••

SWISS FRIED VENISON STEAK

1 pound steak, 1 inch thick
1/4 teaspoon pepper
1 cup water
3 tablespoons chopped onion
1/4 cup flour
3 tablespoons vegetable oil
1 teaspoon salt
3 tablespoons tomato sauce or catsup

Wipe steak dry and pound flour onto meat on both sides. Sprinkle with salt and pepper. Heat oil and brown steaks on both sides. Add remaining ingredients, cover and boil 3 minutes. Then bake at 325°F for 1 hour, basting steaks often.

IOWA VENISON DELIGHT

8 venison steaks, 1/2 inch thick (2-1/2 pounds)
1 teaspoon salt
1/4 teaspoon pepper
1/2 cup margarine or butter
2 small onions, finely chopped
8 medium mushrooms, thinly sliced
8 thin slices boiled ham
8 tablespoons sour cream
2 tablespoons finely chopped parsley

Preheat oven to 350°F. Melt 1/4 cup butter in skillet. Salt and pepper steaks and brown for 10 minutes on each side. Remove meat from skillet and set aside. Melt remaining butter or margarine in skillet and sauté onions and mushrooms until soft and translucent. Remove from heat and prepare 8 pieces of aluminum foil large enough to wrap steak portions generously. On each piece place a steak, topped with a slice of ham, a generous tablespoon of the mushroom-onion mixture, 1 tablespoon sour cream and a pinch of parsley. Wrap packets securely, place on a cookie sheet and bake 25 to 35 minutes or until meat loses all pink color. Serves 8.

••

STEAK WITH GRAPE BRANDY SAUCE

2 pounds venison steak, thinly sliced
3 tablespoons flour
3/4 teaspoon salt
1/4 teaspoon white pepper
3 tablespoons vegetable oil
1 cup heavy cream
Water

In a shallow bowl, mix flour, salt and pepper. Dredge meat in flour mixture and brown on both sides in oil in skillet. Add cream and enough water to almost cover steaks. Cover skillet and simmer for 1 hour. Serve steak with Grape Brandy Sauce. Serves 6 to 8.

Grape Brandy Sauce

2 tablespoons brandy
1/4 teaspoon cinnamon
1 cup grape jelly

In the top part of a double boiler, heat brandy, cinnamon and jelly, stirring until smooth and heated through.

STEAKS

••

HARRIETTE'S BARBECUED STEAK

12 ounces beer
1/2 cup chili sauce
1/4 cup cooking oil
1 tablespoon Worcestershire sauce
1 tablespoon soy sauce
1 tablespoon prepared mustard
1/2 teaspoon Tobasco sauce
1/4 teaspoon liquid smoke
1/2 cup chopped onion
2 cloves garlic, minced
3 pounds venison steak
1 teaspoon salt
1/2 teaspoon pepper

In saucepan mix all ingredients together except steak, salt, pepper and simmer 30 minutes. Brush meat well with sauce. Cook over charcoal briquettes, 20 to 30 minutes per side, or until well done, basting frequently with sauce. Season both sides of steak with salt and pepper during the last few minutes of cooking and serve.

●◆◆

CHEESE FILLED VENISON ROLLS

2 pounds venison round steak
1/4 cup flour
3/4 teaspoon salt
1/4 teaspoon pepper
3/4 cup chopped celery
1/2 cup chopped onion
1 teaspoon finely chopped fresh parsley
2 tablespoon butter
1 cup grated American cheese
1/3 cup soft bread crumbs
3 tablespoons cooking oil
1 cup water
1 1/2 teaspoons instant beef bouillon granules
1/2 teaspoon dry mustard
1/2 teaspoon thyme
1/4 cup cold water
2 tablespoons cornstarch

Cut meat into serving-sized pieces. Mix 1/4 cup flour, salt and pepper. Pound flour mixture into both sides of each piece of meat. Cook celery, onion and parsley in butter until tender but not brown and remove from heat. Stir in cheese and bread crumbs. Spread 1/4 to 1/2 cup cheese mixture on each steak. Roll steaks up, jelly-roll style and secure with toothpicks. Brown steaks in oil. Drain excess oil, then add 1 cup water, bouillon, mustard and thyme. Cover and cook 2 1/2 hours. Blend cold water with cornstarch and stir into pan drippings to make gravy. Serves 6.

STEAKS

••

STEAKS CROWNED WITH VEGETABLES

3 pounds round venison steak
3 tablespoons flour
1/4 teaspoon garlic salt
1/4 teaspoon celery salt
1 teaspoon salt
1/4 teaspoon pepper
1/4 cup shortening
1/3 cup white wine
1 onion, sliced
3 carrots, sliced
3 potatoes, sliced
1 1/2 cups sour cream

Cut meat into serving-sized pieces. Mix flour with garlic salt, celery salt, salt and pepper. Dredge meat in flour mixture and brown well on both sides in shortening. Add wine; cover and simmer 20 minutes. Place steaks in a shallow baking dish and reserve broth. Top each steak with a slice of onion, potato slices and carrot slices. Combine sour cream and reserved wine broth, and pour over steaks. Cover tightly with foil and bake at 300°F for 2 to 2 1/2 hours. Serves 6.

STEAKS

•••

CHOICE LOIN STEAKS

1 pound backstrap steaks
1/2 cup flour
Salt
Pepper
Unseasoned meat tenderizer
Cooking oil

Pound steaks lightly with a meat mallet on both sides. Sprinkle salt, pepper and meat tenderizer on both sides of meat. Heat the oil in a large heavy skillet. Dredge meat in flour and fry in a half-inch of oil 2 to 3 minutes on each side. Serves 2 to 3.

MEDITERRANEAN STEAKS

2 to 3 pounds venison steaks
1/4 teaspoon salt
1/2 teaspoon garlic salt
1 teaspoon dried minced onion
1/8 teaspoon pepper
1 tablespoon lemon juice
10 3/4 ounces canned, condensed cream of mushroom soup
1/4 cup water
1/2 cup dry red wine

Trim any fat from steaks. Place meat in a shallow dish in a single layer. In a bowl, combine salt, garlic salt, minced onion, pepper, lemon juice, mushroom soup, water and wine. Pour over meat. Bake in 325°F oven for 2-1/2 to 3 hours or until very well done. Serves 6.

STEAKS

◆◆

STEAKS FLORENTINE

2 pounds venison steaks (1/2 inch thick)
1/3 cup Italian style salad dressing
1/2 cup yellow cornmeal
Salt and Pepper
Cooking oil

Trim all visible fat from meat. Pour salad dressing over steaks and turn with fork so that each piece is coated with dressing. Marinate, covered, for 1 hour. Remove from marinade and dredge in cornmeal. Salt and pepper each steak. Heat oil in a skillet, and sear meat on both sides. Reduce heat and cook until meat is thoroughly done. Serves 6 to 8.

DOWN-HOME VENISON

2 pounds venison steak cut in serving sized pieces
1/4 cup flour
1 teaspoon salt
1/2 teaspoon pepper
3 tablespoons bacon drippings
1/3 cup chopped celery
3 medium onions, sliced
1 tablespoon Worcestershire sauce
2 cups canned whole tomatoes

Combine flour, salt and pepper in a small bowl. Dredge each piece of meat in flour mixture. In large skillet, brown the meat on both sides in bacon drippings. Add celery, onions and Worcestershire sauce; cook until vegetables are tender. Add undrained tomatoes and simmer, covered 1 1/2 to 2 hours or until meat is tender. Serves 6.

STEAKS

●●

SWISS-STYLE STEAK

1/4 cup flour
1 1/2 pounds round steak (1/2 to 3/4 inches thick)
1/2 teaspoon salt
1/4 teaspoon pepper
1/2 teaspoon garlic salt
2 to 4 tablespoons cooking oil
3 large onions, sliced
1 stalk celery, chopped
1 cup canned whole tomatoes
1 tablespoon Worcestershire sauce
1 tablespoon Teriyaki sauce
1 to 2 tablespoons flour mixed with 2 to 4 tablespoons water

Dredge meat in flour seasoned with salt, pepper and garlic salt. Heat oil in skillet and sear meat until well browned on both sides. Add the remaining ingredients, except flour paste. Bring to a boil, cover and reduce heat. Simmer 1 1/2 hours or until meat is tender. Remove steak from sauce to a platter and thicken sauce slightly with flour-water mixture. Serve sauce separately. Serves 6.

STEAKS

••

NEW ORLEANS VENISON

> 2 pounds venison steak
> 3/4 teaspoon lemon-pepper seasoning
> 1/2 teaspoon salt
> 1/4 teaspoon cayenne pepper
> 1 clove garlic, minced
> 3 slices lime, chopped
> 2 cups chopped onion
> 1 cup chopped green pepper
> 1 teaspoon soy sauce
> 1 cup sauterne
> 1/2 teaspoon parsley flakes

Season meat with lemon-pepper, salt, cayenne pepper and garlic. Place meat in Dutch oven and add rest of the ingredients. Cover, bring quickly to a boil and then reduce heat and simmer until meat is tender, about 1 1/2 to 2 hours. Serves 4 to 6.

CITRUS VENISON STEAKS

> 2 pounds venison steaks
> Juice of 1 lemon, plus 2 to 3 tablespoons lemon juice
> 1/2 teaspoon garlic salt
> 1/2 teaspoon onion salt
> 1/8 teaspoon pepper

Line a shallow baking dish with enough aluminum foil to cover meat while cooking. Place steaks in a single layer on foil. Squeeze the juice from a half lemon over exposed sides of meat and sprinkle with garlic salt, onion salt and pepper. Turn steaks over and season with other half lemon, salts and pepper. Seal aluminum foil around steaks and bake at 400°F for 50 minutes. Uncover steaks; pour 2 to 3 tablespoons lemon juice over meat and broil for 10 minutes. Serves 6 to 8.

ROASTS

A roast may be the toughest, gamiest piece of meat in your freezer. A number of recipes will help make a roast a culinary delight, like this one, Vicky's Venison Roast (see page 68).

A roast can be the gamiest piece of meat you'll ever cook. Because it's in a big chunk, the meat is well sealed by the outer layer and has little contact with seasonings. Punching holes into a roast and stuffing pieces of garlic in is a common trick, but may be ineffective with a gamey roast. Cooking a roast slowly until it is so tender it can be cut with a fork won't alter the gamey taste either.

I like to cook a roast in a crock pot until it's fork tender, which usually takes three to five hours. Along with the meat I add lots of onions, other vegetables and seasonings. (See recipes.) When the roast is done I test it for taste. If it's gamey, I remove it from the pot, shred it to pieces, put it back in the hot, original liquid it was cooked in, and simmer it on low for an hour. That way the juices permeate all the meat pieces and flavor them more thoroughly. If the meat is still gamey (this may be possible with a strong-tasting chunk), then I go to plan B and use the meat in a stroganoff, stew, or chili, where it will be re-flavored with new spices.

I've always found, for some unexplained reason, that a roast always tastes better after it's been refrigerated and eaten another day.

To avoid gamey roasts, do two things: make roasts out of the better cuts of meat, or avoid them altogether if the animal is questionable or taken during the peak of the rut.

ROASTS

◆◆◆

Recipes

ROASTS

◆◆

VICKY'S VENISON ROAST

2 or 3 pound venison roast
1 to 1-1/2 tablespoons lard
salt, pepper, garlic salt
1 to 2 tablespoons flour

Sauce

2 cups hot water
1/4 cup vinegar
3 or 4 bay leaves
1/2 teaspoon allspice
1/2 teaspoon thyme
1 teaspoon celery salt
1/4 cup lemon juice
3/4 cup brown sugar
8 to 10 whole cloves
1/2 teaspoon paprika
2 cups tart chopped apples

Lard venison on all sides, then rub well with salt, pepper, garlic salt and flour. Brown in hot fat turning often to brown all edges. Transfer to large roaster.

Preheat oven to 350°F. Combine sauce ingredients in pan, heat to boiling and pour over meat in roaster being sure to have some apples on top. Cover tightly and cook until tender (about 30 to 35 minutes per pound). Remove cover the last 30 minutes to insure a good brown color to the sauce. Increase proportions for larger roasts.

ROASTS

••

VENISON ROAST WITH CIDER

4 pound venison roast
1 tablespoon cooking oil
1 1/4 teaspoon pepper
1/2 teaspoon salt
1/4 cup flour
1 teaspoon ground oregano
1/2 teaspoon thyme
1 teaspoon rosemary
1/2 teaspoon garlic salt
1 cup apple cider or juice
1 tablespoon lemon juice
1 cup water
Cornstarch

Cut several slits in the roast and rub with oil. In a small bowl, mix pepper, salt, flour, oregano, thyme, rosemary and garlic salt. Add just enough water to make a paste. Rub paste into meat, working into each slit. Place meat in baking dish containing apple cider, lemon juice, and water. Bake uncovered in a 325°F oven for one hour. Baste with juices and cider mixture. Cover. Roast another 2 1/2 hours or until well done, basting every 15 or 20 minutes. Slice thin and make gravy from pan juices by thickening with cornstarch, if desired. (Combine 2 to 3 teaspoons cornstarch with water and then add to pan juices. Cook until thickened.) Serves 6 to 8.

ROASTS

●◆

VENISON ROAST TOPPED WITH STUFFING

3-4 pound venison roast
1/2 cup very soft butter or margarine
2 cups dry breadcrumbs
1 teaspoon salt
1/2 teaspoon pepper
1/2 medium onion, chopped
1 teaspoon sage
1/2 teaspoon dried leaf thyme
1/2 cup chopped celery
1 teaspoon parsley flakes
1 teaspoon basil
1 cup unpeeled and coarsely chopped tart apple
1 beef bouillon cube, dissolved in 1 cup hot water
6 strips bacon

Place roast on a large sheet of heavy-duty aluminum foil. Spread butter or margarine over top and sides of meat. In mixing bowl combine breadcrumbs, salt, pepper, onion, sage, thyme, celery, parsley flakes, basil, apples and bouillon. Mix well. Pat stuffing on top of meat with fingers. Arrange bacon slices on top of stuffing. Fold foil around roast, leaving some air inside but sealing all seams with a double fold. Roast in a 350°F oven for 2 1/2 to 3 1/2 hours or until tender and well done. Slice meat and serve accompanied by stuffing. Serves 8 to 10.

ROASTS

◆◆

SWEET & SOUR VENISON

> 3 pound venison roast
> 6 tablespoons cooking oil
> 1 teaspoon salt
> 1 1/4 cups dark brown sugar
> 2 teaspoons prepared mustard
> 2 tablespoons cider vinegar
> 1/4 cup water

In a Dutch oven sear meat on all sides in hot oil. Combine salt, brown sugar, mustard and vinegar to make a thick paste and spread paste all over roast. Carefully pour water into bottom of pan. Cover roast and bake at 350°F for 2 to 3 hours, or until meat loses all pink color. Baste frequently with pan drippings, adding more water if needed. Serves 6.

VENISON IN BEER

> 4 to 5 pound venison roast
> 3/4 to 1 teaspoon salt
> 1/2 teaspoon pepper
> 6 slices bacon
> 2 beef bouillon cubes
> 1/4 cup boiling water
> 1 onion, sliced
> 2 bay leaves
> 12 ounces beer
> Flour

Salt and pepper roast and place in 9" X 11" pan lined with sufficient aluminum foil to cover roast. Secure bacon on top of meat with toothpicks. Dissolve bouillon cubes in boiling water. Add onion, bay leaves, bouillon and beer. Seal with foil and roast 3 to 3 1/2 hours in a 350°F oven or until completely done. If gravy is desired, thicken pan juices with flour. Serves 6.

ROASTS

••

JELLY GLAZED VENISON ROAST

4 to 5 pound venison roast
8 slices bacon
Salt
Pepper
1/4 cup orange juice
2 tablespoons lemon juice
1/4 teaspoon powdered allspice
2 tablespoons melted margarine
2 tablespoons orange juice
1/4 cup crabapple jelly

Season meat with salt and pepper and cover with bacon. Mix orange juice, lemon juice and allspice together. Sear meat in preheated 450°F oven for 15 minutes. Reduce heat to 350°F and cook uncovered for 4 hours or until meat is well done, basting frequently with juice mixture. Combine margarine, orange juice and jelly, brush meat with glaze and continue roasting uncovered, basting with glaze several times. Serves 10.

ROASTS

◆◆

VENISON WITH SOUR CREAM

   3 to 4 pound venison roast
   2 cups water
   1 bay leaf
   1/8 teaspoon thyme
   1/8 teaspoon basil
   1/4 teaspoon pepper
   3/4 teaspoon salt
   1 large stalk celery, diced
   4 carrots, sliced
   4 small turnips, quartered
   6 small potatoes, quartered
   2 shallots, sliced
   6 slices bacon
   1/2 cup sour cream

Place meat in Dutch oven. Add water, seasonings and vegetables. Lay bacon on top of meat. Cover pan tightly and simmer until vegetables are cooked and meat is tender, 3 to 3 1/2 hours. Remove meat to platter. Add sour cream to pan drippings and heat through, but do not boil. Serve sauce immediately with meat. Serves 8.

ROASTS

••

CURRIED VENISON

1 1/2 medium onions, grated
4 stalks celery, chopped
2 medium apples, grated
4 to 6 tablespoons cooking oil
3 pounds cooked venison roast, cubed
2 teaspoons salt
1/4 teaspoon pepper
1/4 teaspoon garlic powder
2 teaspoons curry powder
2 cups beef broth
1/4 teaspoon ginger
1/8 teaspoon Tabasco sauce
1 tablespoon Worcestershire sauce
2 tablespoons flour
1/4 cup cold water
1 cup milk
1 egg yolk, well beaten

In heavy skillet sauté onions, celery and apples in oil until lightly brown. Add meat, salt, pepper, garlic powder, curry powder, beef broth, ginger, Tabasco and Worcestershire sauce. Mix well. Bring to a boil and simmer, covered, for 20 to 24 minutes. Mix flour to a smooth paste with the water and add a little at a time, stirring mixture constantly until thick. Simmer 5 minutes. Remove from heat and let stand for 1 hour so seasonings can permeate meat. Reheat and add milk and egg yolk gradually, stirring constantly. Heat just to boiling and serve over rice. Serves 8 to 10.

●●◆

BACON ROAST

>3 to 4 pound venison roast
>1/2 teaspoon salt
>1/4 teaspoon pepper
>1/4 teaspoon onion salt
>1/4 teaspoon garlic salt
>1/4 teaspoon oregano
>1/2 teaspoon parsley flakes
>8 slices bacon

Rub seasonings into roast. Secure bacon strips over meat with toothpicks. Wrap meat securely in aluminum and bake at 325°F for 2 1/2 to 3 1/2 hours, or until meat is tender and loses pink color. Serves 6 to 8.

ORANGE BASTED ROAST

>3 or 4 pound venison roast
>1 slice bacon, cut into small pieces
>2 cloves garlic, crushed
>salt and pepper
>1 bay leaf
>2 cloves
>1 cup orange juice

Cut slits in roast and insert small pieces of bacon and garlic. Salt and pepper well. Sear meat on all sides. Put meat in roaster and place bay leaf and cloves on top. Baste with orange juice. Roast in 325°F oven until internal temperature reaches 170 degrees, basting frequently with orange juice.

ROASTS

••

VENISON POT ROAST

Marinade

   1 medium onion, sliced
   2 bay leaves
   1/2 teaspoon leaf oregano
   1/4 teaspoon pepper
   1/2 teaspoon salt
   4 cups red wine
   2 tablespoons olive oil

Marinade Variation

   1 medium onion, sliced
   2 cloves garlic, peeled and halved lengthwise
   1 bay leaf
   1/2 teaspoon dried rosemary
   1/2 teaspoon thyme
   1/4 teaspoon dried basil
   1/4 teaspoon pepper
   4 cups red wine
   3/4 teaspoon salt

Pot Roast

   4 pound venison roast
   4 tablespoons shortening

Prepare one of the marinades shown above by combining the ingredients listed. Marinate meat for 3 hours, turning frequently. Remove meat and pat dry. Brown meat in shortening in large Dutch oven. Roast in slow oven (300°F) for 4 hours or until well done, basting with marinade every 15 to 20 minutes. Serves 8.

ROASTS

••

GREEN CREEK ROAST

Marinade

1/2 cup vinegar
2 cups water
Juice from one lemon
1/2 cup olive oil

Combine above ingredients in glass bowl and marinate roast overnight.

Roast

3 to 4 pound venison roast
1/2 cup dry wine
3/4 to 1 teaspoon salt, or to taste
1 teaspoon pepper
1/2 teaspoon garlic powder
6 thin round slices of fresh lemon
3 strips bacon, cut in half

Rinse roast with water and pat dry. Brush on half the wine and sprinkle with salt, pepper and garlic powder. Place lemon slices on top of roast and top with bacon, secured by toothpicks. Roast in 275°F oven for 4 to 5 hours. Baste often with sauce (see below) while baking. Serves 6 to 8.

Sauce For Green Creek Roast

1/4 cup butter
1/4 cup honey
1/2 cup frozen orange juice concentrate
1/2 teaspoon rosemary

Mix all ingredients together in a small bowl.

ROASTS

••

DELORES' POT ROAST

> 3 or 4 pound venison roast
> 1/8 to 1/4 pound suet, diced
> Salt, pepper, and garlic salt to taste
> 1 small can tomato juice, or 1 can tomato soup
> 1 can water
> 1 bay leaf
> 6 small potatoes
> 4 carrots, chopped
> 1 onion, chopped in quarters

Place roast in heavy pan. Sprinkle with small amount of suet, salt, pepper and garlic salt to taste. Pour tomato juice (or soup) over roast plus 1 can of water. Place bay leaf on roast, cover and bake at 325°F for 2-1/2 to 3 hours. About 45 minutes before roast is done, add potatoes, carrots and onions.

This recipe compliments of Delores Croswell, Washougal, Washington.

ROLLED POT ROAST

> 12 pound rolled roast
> 1 package Au Jus mix
> 1 package onion soup mix
> 1 package mushroom mix
> 2 yellow onions, diced
> 1 quart water
> 8 potatoes, quartered
> 12 carrots, chopped

Brown meat on all sides. Place meat in Dutch oven and add dry mixes, water and onion. Simmer over low heat for 4 hours. Add potatoes and carrots and simmer until vegetables are tender.

ROASTS

◆◆◆

JIM'S VENISON ROAST

2 to 3 pound venison roast
4 cups milk
3 tablespoons shortening
1/4 teaspoon garlic salt
1/4 teaspoon onion salt
1/4 teaspoon salt
1/8 teaspoon pepper
10 3/4 ounces canned condensed cream of chicken soup
10 3/4 ounces water (soup can full)
1/4 cup red wine

Place venison in milk to cover and let soak for at least 1 hour. This mellows stronger venison. Rinse milk from meat. Sprinkle with dry seasonings. Brown meat in shortening over high heat. Mix soup, water and wine and pour over browned meat. Cover and bake at 350°F for 2 hours or until tender. Serves 4.

ROAST WITH BARBECUE SAUCE

3 to 4 pound venison roast
2 tablespoons shortening
1/2 bottle barbecue sauce (use your favorite recipe)

Brown meat in shortening on all sides in a heavy Dutch oven. Cover and bake for 3 to 3 1/2 hours in a 350°F oven, basting with pan drippings from time to time. Pour barbecue sauce over the roast. Serves 6 to 8.

ROASTS

◆◆◆

VENISON ROAST

5 pound venison roast (any cut)
Several strips salt pork
2 cloves garlic, sliced
Salt and pepper
Flour
3 tablespoons olive oil
2 onions, coarsely chopped
2 carrots, sliced
2 stalks celery, chopped
1 small green pepper, chopped
2 potatoes, chopped
1 teaspoon marjoram
1 teaspoon minced parsley
1/2 cup beef bouillon
1/2 cup dry white wine
1/2 cup sour cream
1 tablespoon paprika

Cut several deep slits in roast. Using a knife, push the strips of salt pork into the slits. Cut garlic lengthwise into thin slivers and push also into the slits. Rub the roast with salt and pepper and roll in flour. Sear quickly on all sides in olive oil in a Dutch oven. Add onions, carrots, celery, green pepper, potatoes, marjoram, parsley, bouillon and wine to pot. Cover and simmer for 3 to 3 1/2 hours or until well done, adding more water if necessary. When meat is done remove to a hot platter and add sour cream to broth and heat through. Serve roast with sauce poured over each piece. Sprinkle with paprika for garnish just before serving. Serves 10.

ROASTS

◆◆

CREAMY ROAST VENISON

3 pound venison roast
1/3 cup cider vinegar
3 tablespoons flour
1/2 teaspoon salt
1/4 teaspoon pepper
2 to 3 tablespoons bacon drippings
3 strips bacon, cut in half
1 onion, sliced into rings
1/2 cup hot water
10 3/4 ounces canned condensed cream of mushroom soup
1/3 teaspoon garlic salt
1/4 teaspoon leaf basil

Soak a clean cloth in vinegar and wipe the roast. Sprinkle with salt, pepper, and coat with flour. In Dutch oven, sear meat on all sides in bacon drippings. Lay strips of bacon across roast, securing with toothpicks. Hang the rings of onion slices over the toothpicks. Add the hot water, mushroom soup, garlic salt and basil to Dutch oven. Cover and simmer for 2 to 3 hours or until tender. Thicken pan juices to make gravy if desired. Serves 6 to 8.

ROASTS

•••

ROCKY MOUNTAIN ROAST

**4 to 5 pound venison roast
1 cup light cream
1 teaspoon savory
1 teaspoon finely chopped fresh parsley
1/4 teaspoon basil
1/2 teaspoon salt
1/2 teaspoon garlic salt
1/4 teaspoon pepper
1 onion, sliced
1 cup sliced fresh mushrooms**

Lay roast on large sheet of aluminum foil placed in a shallow baking dish. Pour cream over roast. Sprinkle with savory, parsley, basil, salt, garlic salt and pepper. Add onion and mushrooms. Wrap foil tightly to seal and roast in 350°F oven for 2 1/2 to 3 hours or until well done. Serves 8 to 10.

ROASTS

•••

VENISON & DUMPLINGS

2 pound venison roast
2 tablespoons cooking oil
2 cups whole tomatoes
1/4 cup dry red wine
1/2 teaspoon salt
1/2 teaspoon rosemary
1/2 teaspoon basil
1/2 teaspoon parsley flakes
1/4 teaspoon pepper
1/4 teaspoon garlic salt or 1 clove garlic, finely minced

Brown meat on all sides in oil. Add undrained tomatoes, wine, salt, rosemary, basil, parsley, pepper and garlic salt. Cover and simmer until meat is tender, 2 to 3 hours, adding more water if necessary. Make dumplings (see below) and drop by spoonfuls into cooking meat mixture. Return to boiling. Reduce heat and simmer 12 to 15 minutes. Remove meat and dumplings and serve pan drippings as a sauce with the meal.

Dumplings

1 cup flour
2 tablespoons fresh minced parsley
2 teaspoons baking powder
1/2 teaspoon salt
1 egg
1/4 cup milk
2 tablespoons melted margarine

Mix together flour, parsley, baking powder and salt. Combine egg, milk and melted margarine. Add to flour mixture, stirring just until blended. Then drop by spoonfuls into cooking meat mixture and proceed as directed above.

ROASTS

••

VENISON SAUERBRATEN

3 to 4 pound venison roast
1 teaspoon salt
1/2 teaspoon pepper
2 medium onions
1 medium carrot, sliced
1 large stalk celery, sliced
4 whole cloves
4 crushed peppercorns
2 bay leaves
2 cups cider vinegar
1/4 cup butter or margarine (1/2 stick)
12 small gingersnaps, crushed
1 tablespoon sugar
2 tablespoons flour mixed with 1/4 cup water (optional)

Begin to prepare several days ahead. Season meat with salt and pepper and place in a glazed crock or in a stainless steel or glass bowl. Add onions, carrots, celery, cloves, peppercorn, bay leaves and vinegar. Cover and refrigerate for 3 days, turning several times a day. When ready to cook, drain meat and wipe dry. Strain and reserve marinade. Melt butter in Dutch oven and sear meat on all sides. Add the marinade and bring to a boil. Lower heat and simmer covered 2 to 3 hours or until meat is cooked through and very tender. Remove meat to heated platter and cover with foil to keep warm. Bring pan juices to a boil. Add gingersnaps and sugar. Stir over medium heat until thickened. If necessary, add flour and water mixture as needed, to thicken further and cook until desired thickness is reached. Pour some of the sauce over the sauerbraten, reserving the rest to serve when roast is sliced. Serve with potato dumplings. Serves 6-8. (See next page.)

ROASTS

••

POTATO DUMPLINGS

  6 medium potatoes, peeled and coarsely grated
  4 slices white bread
  1/2 teaspoon salt
  1 cup cold water or milk
  2 tablespoons parsley flakes
  1 medium onion, peeled and coarsely grated
  2 eggs, well beaten
  1/4 cup flour
  2 quarts boiling salted water

Place grated potatoes in a fine sieve and press with paper towels to remove as much moisture as possible. Trim crusts from bread and soak in water or milk for 2 minutes; squeeze out water and mix bread with salt, parsley, onion, potato and eggs. Shape into balls about 1 1/2 inches in diameter. Roll in flour and drop dumplings into boiling water, cover, reduce heat and boil gently for 12 to 15 minutes. Drain in sieve or colander. Serve with sauerbraten.

Soups & Chili Recipes

••

What more could you want on a cold winter night than a hot bowl of soup or chili? Luckily, venison lends itself very well to all sorts of recipes. This one, Sue's Elk Chili, is my favorite (see page 95).

Soups and chili recipes are excellent for utilizing strong and gamey meats, especially chili, because tomato sauce is a superb ingredient that neutralizes the gamey taste. The following recipes are well suited to strong tasting venison, but you can substitute your favorite chili recipe and come up with a satisfying dish.

The same is true with soups, which can be altered to accommodate your tastes. As a tip, I like to toss in smoked pork hock (which can be purchased in any meat market) or a ham bone, or a couple of sausages cut in chunks. Any of these additions will help neutralize gamey venison in your soup pot, and add a zesty flavor.

Soups & Chili Recipes

••

Recipes

Albondigas Soup

2 pounds ground venison
2 eggs
1/2 cup cracker crumbs
1/2 teaspoon salt
1/2 teaspoon white pepper
1/2 teaspoon basil
2 tablespoons vegetable oil
2 small carrots, parboiled and chopped
2 potatoes, parboiled and chopped
4 cups beef broth
2 - 15 ounce cans navy beans
2 cloves garlic, diced
1/2 cup green chilies, diced
1/4 cup jalapeno peppers, diced
1-1/2 cups crushed tomatoes

Combine venison, eggs, cracker crumbs, salt, pepper, and basil. Make meatballs about one inch in diameter. Brown meatballs in oil, drain, and set aside. Parboil potatoes and carrots, then chop. Combine remaining ingredients, add meatballs, potatoes and carrots. Cover and simmer 1 to 1-1/2 hours. Serves 6 to 8.

Soups & Chili Recipes

◆◆

Venison In Soup

1 1/2 pounds venison steaks
1/2 cup Italian bread crumbs
2 tablespoons flour
1/2 teaspoon garlic salt
1/2 teaspoon onion salt
1 can chicken noodle soup (10-3/4 ounces)
1 can water
1 teaspoon A-1 Steak sauce
1 teaspoon Heinz 57 Steak sauce

Slice venison steaks in thin strips 1/4" thick. Shake steak strips in bag with bread crumbs, flour and salts to coat strips. In deep skillet, brown steak strips in hot oil. Remove steak strips from pan and place in casserole dish. Add soup, water, steak sauces and remaining bread crumb mixture to casserole dish. Cover and bake 45 minutes to 1 hour in 300°F oven. Serves 4.

Venison Bean Soup

1 - 20 ounce package of mixed dry beans (Hurst's 15 Beans)
1 pound ground venison
1/2 pound smoked venison sausage cut in 1/2" chunks
2 - ham hocks
1 large onion, chopped
1 large can tomatoes
1 red pepper, chopped
1 teaspoon chili powder
Juice of 1 lemon
1 clove minced garlic
Salt and pepper to taste

Wash beans, cover with water and soak in 2 tablespoons of salt for 12 hours. Drain and add two quarts unsalted water. Brown ground venison and sausage chunks. Add venison, sausage and ham hocks to beans. Bring to a boil, reduce heat and simmer 2-1/2 to 3 hours. Add onion, tomatoes, red pepper, lemon juice and seasonings. Simmer additional 30 minutes. Serves 16.

SOUPS & CHILI RECIPES

◆◆

GROUND VENISON SOUP

2 pounds ground venison
3/4 cup diced onion
4 tablespoons cooking oil
2 cups diced potatoes
1 cup diced carrots
1/2 cup barley
1 cup beef bouillon
1/2 teaspoon thyme
2 bay leaves
1/2 teaspoon salt
1 teaspoon garlic salt
1/4 teaspoon pepper
2 to 2 1/2 quarts water
29 ounces canned whole tomatoes (3 1/2 cups)

Brown meat and onion in oil in a Dutch oven until onions are soft and meat loses its pink color. Add potatoes, carrots, barley, beef bouillon, thyme, bay leaves, salt, pepper, garlic salt, water and tomatoes. Cover and simmer for 1 1/2 to 2 hours. Add more water if necessary. Skim off any excess fat just before serving. Serves 6 to 8.

Note: A great use for deerburger.

SOUPS & CHILI RECIPES

◆◆

ITALIAN MEATBALL SOUP

1 medium onion, chopped
1 clove garlic, minced
2 tablespoons cooking oil
4 cups water
2 1/2 cups condensed beef broth
6 ounces tomato paste
2 medium potatoes, peeled and cubed (2 cups)
2 medium carrots, sliced
1 beaten egg
3 tablespoons fresh parsley, chopped
3/4 teaspoon salt
1/2 teaspoon leaf oregano
1/8 teaspoon pepper
1 pound ground venison
1/4 cup rice

Cook onion and garlic in oil until onion is tender but not brown. Stir in water, broth and tomato paste. Bring to a boil. Add potatoes and carrots and simmer for 5 minutes. In a mixing bowl, combine egg, parsley, salt, oregano and pepper. Add ground venison, and rice and mix well. Form mixture into small balls. Add a few meatballs at time to boiling soup. Reduce heat and simmer about 45 minutes or until meatballs and vegetables are done. Serves 6.

Soups & Chili Recipes

••

Venison & Cheddar Chowder

2 pounds ground venison
1/2 cup chopped onion
3 tablespoons chopped green peppers
1/4 cup chopped celery
4 medium potatoes, peeled and cubed
1 1/2 tablespoons instant beef bouillon granules
1/2 teaspoon salt
2 cups water
3 cups milk
4 tablespoons flour
1 1/3 cups grated cheddar cheese

Brown venison in a large saucepan with onion, green pepper and celery. Add potatoes, beef bouillon granules, salt and water. Cook until vegetables are tender (1/2 hour). Blend 1/2 cup milk with flour. Add to saucepan contents, stirring constantly. Add the rest of milk, stirring constantly. Cook until thickened. Add cheese and stir just until cheese melts. Serve immediately. Serves 6 to 8.

◆◆

Venison Rib Soup

2 1/2 pounds venison ribs
4 quarts water
2 teaspoons salt
1 cup grated onion
1 cup grated carrots
1/2 cup grated potatoes
1/2 cup diced celery
1 teaspoon chopped parsley
1/2 teaspoon marjoram
1/2 teaspoon pepper
10 3/4 ounces condensed tomato soup
2 cups water
1/2 cup small shell macaroni

Place ribs in a large soup kettle with water and salt. Boil at medium heat for one hour and then simmer for about 8 hours. Remove ribs from liquid. Strain liquid and return to kettle. Remove meat from rib bones, and cut into small chunks. Return meat to kettle. Add onion, carrots, potatoes, celery, parsley, marjoram, pepper, tomato soup and 2 more cups water. Boil the contents of kettle for 20 minutes or until vegetables are barely tender. Add macaroni and simmer until macaroni is cooked. Serves 6 to 8.

SOUPS & CHILI RECIPES

•••

BARLEY SOUP DU JOUR

1 1/2 pounds venison bones
1 pound cubed venison
2 1/2 quarts water
3 beef bouillon cubes
1 1/2 teaspoons salt
1 stalk celery, finely diced
1/2 teaspoon pepper
1/8 teaspoon thyme
1 onion, chopped
3 sliced carrots
2 tablespoons finely chopped parsley
1/2 cup barley

Place venison bones, venison, water, bouillon cubes, salt, celery, pepper, thyme and onion in a large pot. Boil for about one hour. Remove bones and skim stock. Boil for about 1 1/2 hours longer. Add carrots and parsley. Boil another 30 minutes, adding more water to keep liquid to about 2 quarts. Add barley. Simmer about 30 to 40 minutes, stirring occasionally. Serves 6 to 8.

Soups & Chili Recipes

◆◆◆

Venison Microwave Minestrone

5 cups water
1 pound venison (any cut) cubed
1 small onion, diced
1 leek, thinly sliced
1/4 teaspoon pepper
1/2 teaspoon sweet basil
1 teaspoon parsley
1/2 cup diced carrots
16 ounces canned whole tomatoes (2 cups)
1/2 cup uncooked spaghetti, broken into 1-inch long pieces
2 medium zucchini (3 to 4 inches long), sliced unpeeled
16 ounces canned kidney beans, drained
1 cup green cabbage, finely shredded
1 teaspoon salt
Parmesan or Romano cheese, grated

In a 4-quart casserole, suitable for a microwave, pour water over meat. Add onion, leek, pepper, basil and parsley. Cover, cook on HIGH in microwave for 25 to 35 minutes or until meat is tender, turning meat a couple of times. Add carrots and tomatoes. Cover and cook on HIGH for 10 minutes. Stir in spaghetti, zucchini, beans, cabbage and salt. Cover and cook on HIGH for another 10 minutes, stirring once. Remove from oven and let stand for 5 minutes. Serve each bowl full topped with grated cheese. Serves 6.

Soups & Chili Recipes

◆◆◆

Sue's Elk Chili

2 cups pinto beans
5 cups canned tomatoes, undrained and chopped
3 green bell peppers, chopped
3 medium onions, chopped
1/4 teaspoon garlic powder
1/2 cup parsley
3 1/2 to 4 pounds ground elk
1/4 cup (scant) red New Mexico chili powder (medium hot powder)
2 tablespoons salt
1 1/2 teaspoons black pepper
1 1/2 teaspoons ground cumin
1 1/2 teaspoons Accent (optional)

Wash beans thoroughly and soak overnight, drain. Cover beans with two inches water, cover and simmer until tender. Add tomatoes and simmer 5 minutes more. In pan, sauté green pepper and onion. Sauté meat with garlic powder and parsley. Add green peppers, onion and meat to beans and tomatoes. Add remaining ingredients. Cover and simmer all for one hour. Remove cover and simmer an additional 30 minutes. Skim off fat if any is present. Makes 4 to 5 quarts. Freezes well.

This recipe compliments of Sue Gooding, Albuquerque, New Mexico.

SOUPS & CHILI RECIPES

◆◆◆

PONCHO'S CHILI

1 package chili seasoning mix
2 tablespoons flour
1 teaspoon salt
4 venison shanks (use boned strips)
1 can (1 pound, 12 ounces) tomatoes
1 can (15 ounces) beans in chili gravy
1 can (15 ounces) golden hominy
1 tablespoons corn meal (optional)

Combine 2 tablespoons chili seasoning mix, flour and salt in a large plastic bag. Add shanks and shake to coat with mixture. In a Dutch oven, brown shanks in oil. Combine remaining chili seasoning with tomatoes and pour over shanks. Simmer, covered, slowly for one hour. Add beans, hominy and corn meal to pan, stirring gently to combine. Continue to cook for 30 minutes or until slightly thickened and meat is tender.

Oven preparation: Slide Dutch oven with browned shanks and tomato mixture into oven. Bake at 325°F for one hour. Proceed as above.

Crock pot preparation: Place browned shanks in crock pot with tomato mixture. Cook on medium for 5 hours. Add beans, hominy and corn meal and continue to cook for 1 hour. If you will be away all day, add all ingredients at the beginning of cooking. The flavors will blend and dinner will be ready when you return.

STEWS

••

A good venison stew will warm your tummy and make you a believer in hunting. Fortunately, stew is easy to manufacture, and allows you to be as creative as you wish, and will also let you use up most edible stuff in your refrigerator or freezer.

Stew meat should be cut up into chunks no bigger than one-inch square. It can be meat from very tough cuts, such as the neck and down around the knees. Cooked long enough, any tough meat will be tenderized so it can be cut with a fork.

Once I shot a mountain goat in Montana, and took out ALL the meat, including the sinewy muscles around the knee joint. Many folks savvy to goat meat said I was crazy, but I chunked that terribly tough meat up, put it in a heavy pot with onions, spices and water, and let it cook all day on my wood stove. It was unbelievably tender and flavorful. You can do the same thing in a crock pot or Dutch oven.

I like to coat stew meat with flour and brown quickly before tossing them in the stew pot. Then, the sky's the limit. Put into the pot anything you like, and cook it so it's tender.

Basically, I like to use chicken broth as the starting liquid in my stew. I make and freeze my own broth by parboiling chickens before barbecuing, frying, or baking them. In the broth I put the meat and lots of onions and celery. After cooking for an hour, I add more spices, and when the meat is almost tender a couple hours later I add potatoes and carrots which will cook in about an hour. Carrots and potatoes, two stew staple ingredients, shouldn't be added at the very beginning because they'll turn to mush if cooked too long.

Don't be afraid to add a variety of meats from your refrigerator to the stew pot, such as leftover chicken, ham scraps, leftover hamburger or whatever other meat you might find. Another interesting variation is to add a cup or two of cooked rice to your stew concoction.

The following recipes are some of my favorites, and I'm sure you'll start experimenting on your own when you realize how good stew can be.

Finally, stew is one medium in which you can neutralize the gamey taste of strong meat because it cooks so long in a highly seasoned liquid.

STEWS

◆◆◆

A good hot stew with everything but the kitchen sink thrown in will make any piece of venison a pleasure to eat. The ingredients pictured above are basics — you can add whatever you have in your pantry or refrigerator. My favorite stew, Western Style Stew, is on page 103).

Recipes

STEWS

◆◆◆

CAMPER'S STEW

2 pounds cubed venison
Salt
Pepper
Flour
4 to 6 tablespoons margarine
2 cups hot water
4 ounces canned mushrooms (1 1/2 cup), undrained
1 medium onion, sliced
8 ounces canned kidney beans (1 cup), undrained
3 medium carrots, sliced crosswise
6 ounces tomato sauce (3/4 cup)
1/2 teaspoon garlic salt
2 bay leaves
1/2 teaspoon leaf oregano

Salt and pepper meat and dredge in flour. Brown in margarine. Add water, vegetables, tomato sauce, garlic salt, bay leaves and oregano. Cover and simmer slowly for two hours or until meat is tender. Serves 6.

••

Unbelievable Ham Stew

    2 cups cooked ham, cut in 1/2" cubes
    2 cups Italian venison sausage
    2 cups chicken broth
    2 cans kidney beans, drained
    1 onion, chopped
    1/2 cup fresh mushrooms, sliced
    1 package Sloppy Joe mix
    1 package dry onion soup mix
    1 cup cooked rice
    3 cooked potatoes, cut in 1" chunks

Cut sausage into 1/2" chunks and brown in oil. In deep pot, combine all ingredients except rice and potatoes and bring to a boil. Reduce heat and simmer 30 minutes. Add rice and potatoes and simmer an additional 15 minutes. Serves 6-8.

Easy Burger Stew

    1 1/2 pounds venison burger
    5 medium potatoes, cut in 1-inch cubes
    4 carrots, cut in 1/2-inch sections
    2 cups cooked rice
    3 to 5 dashes of liquid smoke
    1 package brown gravy mix
    1 package Sloppy Joe mix
    1 tablespoon parsley
    1/2 teaspoon garlic salt
    1/2 teaspoon onion salt

Brown burger until meat loses its pink color. Place carrots and potatoes in stew pot and cover with water. Add gravy and Sloppy Joe mix, liquid smoke and seasonings, and bring to a low boil stirring occasionally. Boil 5 minutes then add browned burger and cook until potatoes and carrots are tender. Serves 6.

Stews

◆◆◆

Hearty Stew

3 strips bacon, cut into small pieces
2 medium onions, diced
2 stalks celery, diced
1 diced green pepper
1 tablespoon cooking oil
2 pounds venison, cut in 1-inch cubes
1/2 teaspoon garlic salt
1/2 teaspoon salt
1/4 teaspoon pepper
1 1/2 quarts water
3 medium potatoes, diced
4 chopped carrots
1 diced rutabaga
10 3/4 ounces condensed cream of mushroom soup
1 cup sautéed coarsely chopped mushrooms
2 tablespoons flour
4 to 5 tablespoons water

In a Dutch oven, brown bacon, onions, celery and green pepper in oil. Add meat, salts and pepper. Continue cooking until meat is browned on all sides. Add 1 quart water and simmer 1 hour. Add vegetables and simmer until meat and vegetables are tender (30 to 45 minutes). Add mushroom soup, remainder of water (2 cups) and sautéed mushrooms. (Sauté mushrooms in 1 tablespoon butter.) Mix flour with the 4 tablespoons of water and add gradually to the stew, stirring constantly as stew thickens. Simmer 5 minutes. Serves 8.

STEWS

••

DUTCH OVEN STEW

2 pounds venison, cubed
3 tablespoons vegetable oil
1 1/2 quarts water
1 bay leaf
1 teaspoon salt
1/2 teaspoon pepper
6 diced potatoes
6 carrots, chopped
6 ounces tomato sauce
3 medium onions, chopped
1 cup shredded cabbage
1/4 cup water
2 tablespoons flour

Brown meat in a Dutch oven in oil. Add 1 quart water, bay leaf, salt and pepper. Cover and simmer about 1 1/2 hours. Add potatoes, carrots, tomato sauce, onions and enough water to cover meat and vegetables (about 1/2 quart, but amount of water depends on the size of your Dutch oven.) Simmer another 30 minutes and add cabbage. Cook about 20 minutes longer. Blend water and flour together to make a paste. Gradually add it to bubbling stew, stirring constantly until thickened. Recover and simmer until all meat and vegetables are tender. Serves 6 to 8.

STEWS

◆◆

WESTERN STYLE STEW

2 sliced onions
2 chopped green peppers
1 cup diced celery
3 tablespoons shortening
2 pounds venison stew meat, 1-inch cubes
1 garlic clove, minced
1 teaspoon salt
16 ounces tomato sauce
1 bay leaf
2 teaspoons chopped green chilies (optional)
2 cups water
3 diced potatoes
1 small turnip, diced
6 chopped carrots
1/4 cup water and 3 tablespoons flour, mixed into a smooth paste

Sauté onions, peppers and celery in shortening. Add meat, and salt. Brown meat on all sides, stirring frequently. Add tomato sauce, bay leaf, green chilies, and water. Simmer 3 to 4 hours. Add potatoes, turnip and carrots. Thicken to desired consistency with flour and water paste. Simmer 1 hour, or until vegetables are tender. Serves 6 to 8.

◆◆

VENISON & SWEET POTATO STEW

2 pounds venison steak, cubed
2 tablespoons cooking oil
3 medium sweet potatoes, peeled and cubed
2 cups canned whole tomatoes
1 onion, chopped
1 green pepper, chopped
1/8 teaspoon nutmeg
1/4 teaspoon cinnamon
1 clove garlic, minced
1 teaspoon salt
1/2 teaspoon pepper
2/3 cup water
1 cup canned corn
1 zucchini, sliced
2 cups canned peach slices

In a Dutch oven, brown meat in oil. Add sweet potatoes, tomatoes, onion, green pepper, nutmeg, cinnamon, garlic salt and pepper. Add water and mix well. Bake uncovered for 1 1/2 hours at 350°F. Add corn and zucchini and bake 45 minutes longer. Drain peaches and add to stew. Stir well and heat through. Let stand for 5 minutes before serving. Serves 6 to 8.

STEWS

◆◆◆

HACKMAN'S HIGH CAMP STEW

5 pounds round steak, cut in 1-inch cubes
4 tablespoons butter or oil
1 package Au Jus gravy mix
1 package onion gravy mix
1 package mushroom gravy mix
1 package stew seasoning mix
1 1/2 quarts water
2 cans (28 ounces each) tomatoes, diced
1 can (28 ounces) tomato sauce
4 medium onions, diced
8 carrots, diced
8 sticks of celery, diced
3 turnips, chopped
1 parsnip, chopped
1 #303 can corn
1 large head cabbage, chopped
6 large potatoes, diced
Salt & pepper to taste

Brown round steak in butter or oil. In number 10 Dutch oven or large pot, add gravy and seasoning mixes to water, mix. Add round steak and all remaining ingredients except potatoes to pot and bring to a boil. Cover and reduce heat to simmer for 30 to 40 minutes depending on tenderness of meat. Add potatoes and cook until tender.

STEWS

◆◆◆

SUZY'S STEW

5 pounds venison burger
2 green peppers, chopped
1 to 1-1/2 onions, chopped
5 stalks celery, diced
1 large can kidney beans and juice
1 or 2 cans chili beans and juice
2 cans whole green chilies
3 large cans whole tomatoes
1 can corn
1 tablespoon cumin
2 tablespoons chili powder
1/2 teaspoon cayenne pepper
salt to taste

Sauté burger, peppers, onion and celery until meat loses its pink color. Add remaining ingredients, cover and cook 1 hour.

This recipe compliments of Suzy Stockton, Stockton Outfitters, Wise River Montana.

◆◆

DEERBURGER STEW

   1 1/2 to 2 pounds deerburger
   2 tablespoons cooking oil
   1/4 pound bacon
   3 potatoes, diced
   1 tablespoon parsley
   1 onion, diced
   1 can cream of mushroom soup
   1 package brown gravy mix
   1 can kidney beans
   1/2 teaspoon garlic salt
   1/2 teaspoon black pepper
   1 teaspoon A-1 sauce
   1/4 cup red wine, optional

Brown bacon and set aside. Brown burger in oil. Boil potatoes and onion until cooked. Stir gravy mix into cream of mushroom soup. Add all ingredients to potato water and mix well. Simmer 10 minutes.

◆◆◆

LAZY DAY STEW

2 large potatoes, sliced
1 medium onion, chopped
1 celery stalk, diced
1/2 teaspoon salt
1/4 teaspoon pepper
15 ounces canned pork and beans (2 cups)
1 pound ground venison
10 3/4 ounces condensed tomato soup

Place potatoes, onion and celery in the bottom of a greased casserole dish. Sprinkle with half the salt and pepper. Spread pork and beans over vegetables and place ground venison over beans. Sprinkle meat with remaining salt and pepper. Top with tomato soup. Cover and bake 2 to 2 1/2 hours at 350°F or until meat and vegetables are thoroughly cooked. Serves 4.

BARBARA'S SWEET STEW

1 1/2 pounds venison, cut into 1-inch cubes
Salt
Pepper
3 tablespoons butter or margarine
1 teaspoon chili powder
4 tablespoons sweet red wine
2 tablespoons red currant jelly
1/2 teaspoon parsley flakes
1/2 cup water

Sprinkle meat with salt and pepper. Brown meat in butter in a Dutch oven. Sprinkle chili powder on meat. Stir in wine, jelly, parsley flakes, and water. Cover and simmer 1 1/2 hours or until meat is tender, adding more water if necessary. Serves 4.

STEWS

••

CABBAGE & POTATO POTTAGE

2 pounds venison, cubed
10 3/4 ounces condensed tomato soup
1/2 teaspoon salt
1/8 teaspoon pepper
1/4 cup finely chopped celery
3/4 cup water
3 medium potatoes, diced
1/2 cup chopped red cabbage
1/2 cup chopped green cabbage
1/2 cup chopped parsnips
1/2 cup chopped onion
1 tablespoon sugar
2 tablespoons quick cooking tapioca

Mix all ingredients in a Dutch oven. Cook and bake in oven at 250°F for 4 to 5 hours or until meat is tender. Add more water if needed. Serves 6.

LAYERED STEW

1 pound venison, cut in 1-inch cubes
2 stalks celery, diced
2 carrots, diced
1 onion, diced
3 potatoes, diced
1 cup beef bouillon
1 cup tomato juice
1/2 teaspoon coarse ground pepper
1 bay leaf
2 tablespoons tapioca

In Dutch oven, layer meat, celery, carrots, onion and potatoes in order listed. Add remaining ingredients, cover and cook 3 to 4 hours. For a larger stew, use quantities above for each pound of stew meat.

This recipe compliments of Suzy Stockton, Stockton Outfitters, Wise River Montana.

●●

CONNOISSEUR'S VENISON STEW

Marinade

    2 cups dry red wine
    Juice of 1 lemon
    2 large bay leaves
    2 whole cloves
    1 large yellow onion, peeled & sliced
    3 carrots, peeled and chopped
    2 celery stalks, chopped
    1 large garlic clove, peeled & crushed
    Pinch of dried thyme
    1 teaspoon fresh ground black pepper
    1/2 teaspoon salt

Stew

    3 pounds venison, cut in 1-inch cubes
    8 tablespoons sweet butter
    2 tablespoons gin
    3 tablespoons lean salt pork, cut into 1/4" pieces
    1/4 pound fresh mushrooms, remove stems
    12 to 18 tiny pearl onions
    6 chicken livers (optional)
    Salt and pepper to taste

Combine marinade ingredients in large glass bowl and stir well. Add venison, cover and refrigerate for one day. Turn meat once or twice in the marinade. Remove meat from marinade and dry thoroughly with paper towels. Reserve marinade.

Melt 2 tablespoons butter in heavy skillet. Brown venison a few pieces at a time, transfer to bowl with slotted spoon. Add additional butter to pan as needed. Transfer all venison to a flame proof casserole. In a small sauce pan, warm the gin, then pour it over the venison and ignite. Shake the casserole slightly until flames die out.

STEWS

••

Connoisseur's Venison Stew (continued)

Sauté the salt pork in a small skillet until golden brown. Transfer to casserole with slotted spoon. Melt 4 tablespoons butter in small skillet. Add mushroom caps and season with salt and pepper. Cook, stirring occasionally, until tender, about 5 minutes. Transfer mushrooms and cooking liquid to the casserole. Bring 1 quart salted water to a boil, drop in pearl onions and cook 1 minute. Drain and transfer to bowl of ice water; when cool, peel and add to casserole.

Strain the marinade and add it to the casserole; stir well. Set casserole over medium heat; bring to boil; cover and reduce heat to simmer. Cook 40 minutes to 1 hour. (Cooking time depends on tenderness of meat.)

Meanwhile, melt remaining 2 tablespoons butter in small skillet and cook chicken livers until firm but still pink inside, about 5 minutes. Chop into large pieces.

When venison is tender, add livers to casserole (optional). Combine 2 tablespoons of cornstarch with 1/4 up cold water and stir into casserole. Continue stirring until juices thicken. Correct seasonings. Serve over wide noodles or ziti.

Note: stew keeps well when frozen. Freeze small portions and serve for a quick dinner!

◆◆

HUNGARIAN-STYLE VENISON GOULASH

3 pounds venison, cubed
1/2 cup flour
1/4 cup margarine
2 medium onions, diced
1 tablespoon paprika
1 teaspoon salt
1/4 teaspoon pepper
1 cup water
1 tablespoon tomato paste
1 green pepper, diced
1 1/2 cups sour cream

Dredge meat in flour and set aside. Melt margarine in Dutch oven and sauté onions. Add meat and brown over medium heat. Season with paprika, salt and pepper. Stir 3 tablespoons water, tomato paste and green pepper into meat. Cover. Bring to a boil, then lower heat and simmer 2 to 2 1/2 hours or until meat is tender. Check every 30 minutes, and add water as needed to prevent sticking. When meat is tender, add sour cream and heat through over low heat, stirring constantly. Serve over rice. Serves 6 to 8.

STEWS

◆◆

HUNTER'S MOUNTAIN MEAL

1 1/2 pounds venison, cut in 1-inch cubes
1 large onion, finely chopped
2 stalks celery, diced
3 tablespoons vegetable oil
1/2 cup raw rice
10 3/4 ounces canned condensed cream of chicken soup
10 3/4 ounces canned condensed cream of mushroom soup
4 ounces canned, sliced mushrooms
4 teaspoons soy sauce
Dash salt
Pepper
1 cup peas
1 cup water
1/4 cup dry red wine

Brown venison, onion and celery in butter in a Dutch oven. In a large bowl mix together rice, canned soups, mushrooms, soy sauce, salt and pepper. Add to Dutch oven and mix. Add peas, water and wine. Simmer slowly for 1 to 1 1/2 hours. Serves 6 to 8.

STEWS

◆◆

ROMAN-STYLE VENISON

2 pounds venison, cubed
1/2 teaspoon salt
1/4 teaspoon pepper
2 tablespoons flour
5 tablespoons margarine
1 cup hot water
4 ounces canned mushrooms
1 medium onion, sliced
8 ounces canned kidney beans, drained
3 medium carrots, diced
2 cups whole tomatoes
1/2 teaspoon dried oregano

Season meat with salt and pepper and dredge in flour. Brown meat in margarine in a Dutch oven. Add water, mushrooms, onion, beans, carrots, tomatoes and oregano. Cover and simmer slowly for 2 hours or until meat is tender. Serves 6.

GROUND MEAT DISHES

Venison burger can be used in literally hundreds of recipes. It's easily flavored with spices and herbs, rendering even the gamiest meats into a pleasant repast. This recipe, Bell Peppers Stuffed With Venison, (page 123) is sure to please.

Some folks think that just because you grind gamey venison the result will be milder meat if you simply add suet to the ground burger. That's not so. Without exception, I flavor all my burger with spices and seasonings (for detailed information see the section on Burger in Chapter 3, From Field to Freezer).

I cut up all my own game unless I don't have time between hunts. In that case I'll take the carcass to a meat processor. When commercially done I will still spice the burger before cooking it.

When used in chili recipes, soups, casseroles, and meatloafs, ground meat quickly loses its gamey flavor when properly seasoned.

The following recipes were chosen in part because they absorb the seasonings which are needed to neutralize gamey venison.

GROUND MEAT DISHES

◆◆

Recipes

GROUND MEAT DISHES

◆◆◆

TOMATO GOULASH FOR A CROWD

5 pounds ground venison
2 medium onions, chopped
1 large green pepper, chopped
1/2 cup cooking oil
2 - #303 cans stewed tomatoes, mashed
2 - #303 cans tomato sauce
1 - #303 can sweet corn
1 tablespoon sugar
Salt and pepper to taste
2 pounds macaroni

Brown ground meat, onions and pepper in oil stirring constantly; drain excess fat. Mash stewed tomatoes and add to ground meat. Stir in tomato sauce, corn, sugar, salt and pepper. Cover and simmer for one hour using very large pan.

Cook macaroni until tender but not completely done, drain and add to meat and sauce. Simmer for 10 to 15 minutes. Serve with garlic toast.
Serves 10 to 12.

GROUND MEAT DISHES

◆◆

VENISON CORN BAKE

1 pound ground venison
1 tablespoon cooking oil
1 small onion, chopped
1 stalk celery, minced
16-ounce can whole kernel corn (2 cups)
1/2 teaspoon salt
1/4 teaspoon garlic salt
1/2 teaspoon parsley flakes, crushed
2 eggs
1/2 cup cornmeal

Brown venison in oil. When cooked through, add onion, celery, corn and salts, and cook 10 minutes more. Combine eggs and cornmeal, and add to meat mixture. Cook another 15 minutes. Pour mixture into greased loaf pan and bake 30 to 45 minutes at 350°F. Slice and serve with your favorite brown gravy. Serves 4.

GROUND MEAT DISHES

◆◆◆

VENISON CORNBREAD SQUARES

1 to 2 tablespoons cooking oil
1 pound ground venison
1/4 cup diced onion
1/4 cup diced green pepper
1 clove garlic, minced
1 teaspoon chili powder
1/2 teaspoon salt
3/4 cup grated American cheese
2 tablespoons cold water
2 teaspoons cornstarch
1 cup canned tomatoes, cut up
2 tablespoons canned green chilies, diced
1 teaspoon Worcestershire sauce

Preheat oven to 350°F. In a skillet, heat oil and cook venison, onion, green pepper, garlic, chili powder and salt until meat is brown. Set aside. Prepare cornbread batter recipe below. Pour half the batter in a greased 8 X 12 X 2 inch baking dish. Spoon venison mixture over batter. Sprinkle with cheese. Spread remaining batter over cheese. Bake uncovered for 30 to 35 minutes until cornbread is done. Let stand for 5 minutes before cutting into squares. In a small saucepan, blend cold water with cornstarch until smooth. Stir in undrained tomatoes, chilies, and Worcestershire sauce. Cook and stir until thickened. Serve sauce over cornbread squares. Serves 6.

Cornbread Batter

1 cup sifted all-purpose flour
4 teaspoons baking powder
1 cup yellow cornmeal
1 cup milk

1/4 cup sugar
3/4 teaspoon salt
2 eggs
1/4 cup softened shortening

Sift flour with sugar, baking powder and salt. Stir in cornmeal. Add eggs, milk and shortening. Beat until almost smooth, do not over beat.

GROUND MEAT DISHES

MEXICALI PIE

    1 1/2 pounds ground venison
    1 tablespoon cooking oil
    1 minced garlic clove
    1 tablespoon minced onion
    1 finely chopped celery stalk
    3/4 teaspoon salt
    1 to 2 tablespoons chopped green chilies
    1/4 teaspoon oregano
    1/4 teaspoon cumin
    1/4 cup ketchup
    1/2 cup water
    1/2 cup grated cheddar cheese
    2 cups mashed potatoes

Brown ground venison in skillet with oil, garlic, onion, celery, and salt. When meat is brown, add green chilies, oregano, cumin, ketchup and water. Simmer 10 minutes. Put meat mixture in shallow baking dish. Sprinkle cheddar cheese over meat. Spread mashed potatoes on top. Bake at 350°F for 20 to 25 minutes. Serves 4 to 5.

GROUND MEAT DISHES

SPAGHETTI PIE

8 ounces uncooked spaghetti
3 tablespoons margarine
3 beaten eggs
1/2 cup grated Parmesan cheese
1 1/3 cups cream style cottage cheese
1 1/2 pounds ground venison
1 tablespoon cooking oil
1/2 teaspoon garlic salt
3 cups canned tomato sauce (24 ounces)
1/2 teaspoon parsley flakes
1 teaspoon leaf oregano
1/3 teaspoon leaf basil
3/4 cup grated mozzarella cheese

Cook spaghetti in saucepan according to directions on package. Drain. Place in a mixing bowl and stir margarine into hot spaghetti. Stir in eggs and Parmesan cheese; mix well. Place in a greased deep-dish pie pan to form a "crust" for the pie. Spread cottage cheese over spaghetti. In skillet, brown venison in oil, adding garlic salt, until meat loses all pink color. Stir in tomato sauce, parsley, oregano and basil. Simmer 10 minutes. Turn meat into spaghetti crust. Bake uncovered at 350°F for 20 minutes. Sprinkle with mozzarella cheese and bake 10 minutes longer. Serves 5 to 6.

GROUND MEAT DISHES

◆◆◆

PORK & VENISON PIE

> 1 pound ground venison
> 1/4 pound ground fresh pork
> 1/8 pound ground pork sausage
> 1 large onion, finely chopped
> 2 eggs
> 1 teaspoon salt
> 1/2 teaspoon pepper
> 1 cup oatmeal
> 1 tablespoon milk
> 2 Pie Pastry crusts

In a large mixing bowl, mix all ingredients thoroughly. Place in a large heavy skillet and cook until meat loses its pink color. Place meat mixture in unbaked pastry shell (recipe below). Cover with top crust, crimp edges, trim excess, and cut several slits in top crust to allow steam to escape. Brush crust with milk. Bake at 400°F for 20 minutes. Serves 6.

Pie Pastry

> 2 cups all-purpose flour (sift flour before measuring)
> 1 teaspoon salt
> 1/2 cup cooking oil
> 4 to 5 tablespoons cold milk

Sift together flour and salt. Pour cooking oil and cold milk into measuring cup and add all at once to flour mixture. Stir carefully and form into ball. Divide in half and roll out on floured board to fit pie pan.

GROUND MEAT DISHES

••

BELL PEPPERS STUFFED WITH VENISON

1 pound ground venison
1/4 pound ground pork
1/2 cup cooked rice
2 garlic cloves, minced
1/4 cup grated onion
1/2 teaspoon garlic salt
1/4 teaspoon salt
1/8 teaspoon pepper
2 eggs
5 to 6 medium green bell peppers
2 cups tomato sauce
1 bay leaf

Mix venison, pork, rice, garlic, onion, salts, pepper and eggs in bowl. Cut off the tops of the peppers and set aside. Clean out seeds carefully. Stuff meat mixture into peppers and replace tops. Place in a Dutch oven and add tomato sauce and bay leaf. Cover and bring to boil. Simmer on low for about 1 hour. Add water as necessary if liquid gets low. Remove and serve hot. Serves 5 to 6.

GROUND MEAT DISHES

STUFFED WINTER SQUASH

1 medium Acorn squash
1/2 teaspoon salt
2 tablespoons cooking oil
1/2 pound ground venison
3 tablespoons chopped onion
1 stalk celery, finely chopped
2 tablespoons flour
1/4 teaspoon salt
1/4 teaspoon pepper
1 tablespoon chopped parsley
1/2 teaspoon poultry seasoning
2/3 cup milk
3/4 cup cooked rice
1/4 cup grated cheddar cheese

Wash and cut squash in half lengthwise. Scoop out and discard seeds. Sprinkle each half with 1/4 teaspoon of salt Place squash halves cut side down on greased baking dish. Bake at 350°F for 40 to 50 minutes. Meanwhile, add oil to a skillet and brown ground venison with onion, and celery, cooking until meat loses all pink color. Stir in flour, salt, pepper, parsley, and poultry seasoning. Add milk. Cook and stir until mixture comes to a boil. Stir in rice. Remove from heat. Place cooked squash, cut side up, in greased baking dish. Fill each half with meat mixture. Bake 30 minutes more at 350°F or until squash is cooked through. Remove from oven. Top with cheese and bake 2 to 5 minutes or until cheese is melted.
Serves 4 to 5.

GROUND MEAT DISHES

••

TEXAS TACO LOAF

1 1/2 pounds ground venison
1 cup crushed taco-flavored corn chips
2/3 cup grated cheddar cheese
1/2 cup finely chopped onion
1/3 cup finely chopped green pepper
1 teaspoon chili powder
1 egg
1 cup evaporated milk
1 teaspoon salt

In a large bowl, mix all ingredients together thoroughly. Turn into a greased 2-quart covered casserole, spreading evenly around dish. Cover. Bake at 350°F for 1 hour. Serves 4 to 5.

WINEBURGERS

1 1/2 pounds ground venison
4 tablespoons red wine
3 tablespoons bread crumbs
6 strips bacon
2 to 3 tablespoons melted butter
Salt
Pepper

Mix meat with wine and bread crumbs. Refrigerate 1 to 2 hours. Shape into 6 patties. Wrap a strip of bacon around each, securing it with a toothpick. Brush patties with melted butter. Sprinkle with salt and pepper. Grill over coals or broil, basting with butter.

GROUND MEAT DISHES

◆◆

SWISS BURGERS SUPREME

1 1/2 pounds ground venison
2 beaten eggs
1/4 cup milk
3/4 teaspoon salt
1 teaspoon Worcestershire sauce
1/4 teaspoon pepper
2 1/4 cups mashed potatoes
2/3 cup sour cream
1/4 cup chopped green onions
2 tablespoons chopped pimiento
1/2 teaspoon salt
6 slices Swiss cheese

In a mixing bowl, combine eggs, milk, 3/4 teaspoon salt, Worcestershire sauce and pepper. Add meat and mix well. Form into 12 patties. Place one patty in each of 6 individual greased casserole dishes. In other bowl mix potatoes in sour cream, onions, pimiento and 1/2 teaspoon salt. Spoon potato mixture over patties. Top each casserole with one of the remaining patties. Bake uncovered at 375°F for 45 minutes. Top each patty with a slice of cheese and bake two minutes longer or until cheese is melted. Serves 6.

GROUND MEAT DISHES

••

MARINATED BACON BURGERS

1 1/2 pounds ground venison
1/2 to 1 teaspoon salt
1/4 teaspoon pepper
6 slices bacon

Marinade

1/4 cup vegetable oil
1/4 cup soy sauce
2 tablespoons ketchup
1 tablespoon wine vinegar
2 cloves garlic, minced
1/4 teaspoon pepper

In a bowl mix oil, soy sauce, ketchup, vinegar, garlic, and 1/4 teaspoon pepper together. In another bowl mix meat, salt and 1/4 teaspoon pepper together. Shape into 6 patties and place in glass dish. Pour marinade mixture over meat. Cover and refrigerate for 30 to 60 minutes, turning occasionally. Remove patties from marinade. Wrap a strip of bacon around outside edges of each patty and secure with toothpicks. Cook over coals or broil until done.

GROUND MEAT DISHES

MUSHROOM STUFFED DEER LOAF

2 pounds ground deer venison
3/4 cup bread crumbs
1/2 teaspoon sage
1/2 teaspoon basil
1/2 to 1 teaspoon celery salt
2 teaspoons parsley flakes
1 beaten egg
1/2 cup mushrooms, sautéed
1/3 cup beef bouillon
1/3 cup chopped green onions
1/4 cup chopped toasted almonds
2 tablespoons margarine, melted
1 teaspoon lemon juice
1 teaspoon salt
1/2 teaspoon pepper

Combine bread crumbs, sage, basil, celery salt, parsley, egg, sautéed mushrooms, bouillon, onions, almonds, margarine and lemon juice in a bowl until well mixed. Mix salt and pepper with venison. Divide meat in half. Pat half of the meat into a rectangle on a piece of greased 12 X 24 inch aluminum foil. Spoon stuffing mix along center. Cover with remaining meat, pinching edges to seal. Wrap entire meat loaf in foil. Bake at 350°F for 45 minutes or until meat loses pink color. Serves 6.

GROUND MEAT DISHES

••

MEATLOAF CHEESE SURPRISE

    2 pounds ground venison
    1/2 cup diced onion
    1 egg
    4 slices bread
    1 teaspoon salt
    1/2 teaspoon black pepper
    1/4 teaspoon ground sage
    Cheddar cheese, cubed to 1/2" x 1-1/2" square pieces
    3 cans cream of mushroom soup

Wet bread with water or milk and squeeze out most of the liquid (wet bread mixes more thoroughly into the meat). Mix well the ground meat, onion, egg, bread, and seasonings. Using 1/3 to 1/2 cup meat mixture, make an oval meatball. Push a piece of cheese into the center of the meatball being sure the meat covers all the cheese. Flatten meatball into a thick patty and brown in a hot fry pan or Dutch oven that has been sprayed with non-stick spray. (If meat is very lean use a small amount of oil to brown the meat patties.) Put browned patties into a three quart casserole or Dutch oven in a single layer and cover with soup. Cover and bake at 350°F for 45 to 60 minutes, or until soup has blended well with meat juices. Serve with rice, or mashed or baked potatoes.

Note: The cream of mushroom soup may be substituted with cream of chicken or tomato soup.

This recipe compliments of Bruce & Elaine Koffler, Koffler Boats, Junction City, Oregon

GROUND MEAT DISHES

••

ITALIAN STYLE MEATLOAF

1 pound ground venison
6 ounces hot Italian pork sausage or spicy venison sausage
1 can (14 1/2 ounces) Italian style stewed tomatoes
1 cup bread crumbs
1/2 cup chopped onion
1/2 cup chopped green pepper
1 tablespoon parsley
1/2 teaspoon sweet basil
1 egg, beaten

In large bowl, combine all ingredients; mix well. Place in 4-1/2" x 8" loaf pan. Bake at 375°F for 1 hour, drain excess fat. Serves 6.

GROUND MEAT DISHES

◆◆

SAVORY MEATLOAF

2 pounds ground venison
1 pound ground fresh pork
1 1/2 cups crushed saltine crackers
3/4 cup Chili Sauce
2 eggs
1 large onion, chopped
1 1/2 teaspoons salt
1/2 teaspoon pepper
1/4 cup chopped green pepper
1/4 teaspoon garlic powder
4 teaspoons Worcestershire sauce
1/2 teaspoon dried savory

Preheat oven to 350°F. Combine all ingredients in a large mixing bowl. Mix well and turn into 2 greased loaf pans. Bake for 1 to 1 1/2 hours or until meat loses all pink color and is well browned. Serves 6-8.

GROUND MEAT DISHES

TANGY MEATLOAF

2 pounds ground venison (deer)
1/3 pound pork sausage
1 medium onion, diced
2 eggs
1 green pepper, diced
1/2 teaspoon garlic salt
1/2 teaspoon salt
1/4 teaspoon pepper
1 cup dry bread crumbs
1/2 cup brown sugar
1/4 cup cider vinegar
2 cups tomato sauce
2 teaspoons soy sauce
2 teaspoons mustard

In a large bowl mix venison, sausage, onion, eggs, green pepper, garlic salt, salt, pepper and bread crumbs together. In a small bowl mix brown sugar, vinegar, tomato sauce, soy sauce and mustard. Mix meat mixture with 1 1/4 cups tomato sauce mixture. Form into a loaf and place in shallow baking dish. Pour remaining sauce mixture over loaf and bake at 350°F for about one hour. Serves 4 to 6.

GROUND MEAT DISHES

••

VENISON MEATBALLS

2 tablespoons butter
3 tablespoons chopped onion
1 1/2 cups soft bread crumbs soaked in 3/4 cup milk
1 pound ground venison
1/4 teaspoon nutmeg
1/8 teaspoon pepper
1 teaspoon parsley flakes
1/2 teaspoon salt
1 egg
2 tablespoons vegetable oil
1 cup beef broth
1 tablespoon cornstarch
2 to 3 tablespoons cold water

Melt butter in a heavy skillet and sauté onion until transparent. Place onion and butter in mixing bowl along with milk-soaked bread crumbs. Add ground venison, nutmeg, pepper, parsley, salt and egg. Mix well and form into 1-inch balls. Brown meatballs in oil. Add beef broth, cover and simmer for 20 to 30 minutes. Remove meatballs. Mix cornstarch with cold water to form a paste, then add to broth and simmer until sauce thickens. Return meatballs to sauce and heat through. Serves 6.

GROUND MEAT DISHES

SOUR CREAM MEATBALLS

1 1/2 pounds ground venison
1/2 cup minced onion
3/4 cup fine dry bread crumbs
1 tablespoon minced parsley
1 1/2 teaspoon salt
1/8 teaspoon black pepper
1 teaspoon Worcestershire sauce
1 egg
1/2 cup milk
1/4 cup oil

Sour Cream Gravy

1/4 cup flour
1 teaspoon paprika
1/2 teaspoon salt
1/8 teaspoon pepper
2 cups boiling water
3/4 cup sour cream

Combine ground venison, onion, bread crumbs, parsley, salt, pepper, Worcestershire sauce, egg and milk; mix thoroughly. Shape into balls the size of a walnut and brown in oil. Remove meatballs from oil and set aside. Make gravy in remaining oil in pan by adding 1/4 cup flour, paprika, salt and pepper to taste. Stir in 2 cups boiling water and sour cream. Return meatballs to gravy mixture and simmer 15 to 20 minutes. Serves 6 to 8.

This recipe compliments of Delores Croswell, Washougal, Washington

GROUND MEAT DISHES

●●

MEDITERRANEAN MEATBALLS

2 pounds ground venison
2 large apples, peeled and shredded
2 lightly beaten eggs
2 medium onions, chopped
1 teaspoon salt
1/2 teaspoon pepper
4 tablespoons vegetable oil
1 1/2 cups dry red wine
1 3/4 cups water
6 ounces tomato paste
1 teaspoon crumbled basil leaf
1/2 teaspoon crumbled rosemary leaf

Combine venison, apples, eggs, one cup of onion, salt and pepper in a large bowl. Mix lightly. Shape into 1-inch balls. Heat oil in large skillet and brown meatballs on all sides. Remove meatballs from skillet when they are completely browned. Add remaining onion to skillet, sauté, stirring often until golden. Stir in wine, water, tomato paste, basil and rosemary. Add meatballs. Bring to a boil and simmer 10 minutes. Serve with hot rice.
Serves 4 to 6.

GROUND MEAT DISHES

PORCUPINE MEATBALLS

1 pound ground venison
1/2 cup onion, finely chopped
1/2 teaspoon salt
1 teaspoon pepper
1 3/4 cups cooked rice, (or 1/2 cup uncooked instant rice)
2 tablespoons vegetable oil
2 cups tomato sauce
1 teaspoon parsley flakes
1/4 teaspoon garlic salt
1/2 teaspoon crumbled basil

Mix ground venison, onion, salt, pepper, rice, and 1/2 cup tomato sauce. Shape meat mixture into 1-inch balls. Heat oil in a skillet and lightly brown meatballs on all sides. Remove and place in large casserole. Add remaining 1-1/2 cups tomato sauce, parsley, garlic salt and basil. Cover and bake at 350°F for one hour. Serves 4 to 5.

GROUND MEAT DISHES

◆◆◆

MOUNTAIN MEATBALLS

1 1/2 pounds ground venison burger
2 large carrots, grated
1 large potato, grated
1 small onion, grated
1 egg
2 to 3 tablespoons flour
1/4 teaspoon salt (or more to taste)
dash pepper
1 can cream of mushroom soup
10-1/2 ounces of milk (one soup can full)

Mix burger, carrots, potato, onion, egg, flour, salt, and pepper together in a large mixing bowl. Shape into balls about the size of ping pong balls. Fry in a heavy skillet containing sufficient cooking oil to prevent sticking. When meatballs are well browned and cooked through, place them in a greased casserole dish. Pour mushroom soup diluted with milk over meat. Bake in covered casserole dish at 350°F for 35 to 40 minutes. Serves 4-6.

GROUND MEAT DISHES

◆◆◆

MIDWEST MEATBALLS

1 pound ground venison
1/2 pound ground fresh pork
1/4 cup flour
1 small onion, grated
1/4 teaspoon garlic salt
3/4 teaspoon pepper
2 eggs
1 cup milk
1 to 2 tablespoons butter

In mixing bowl combine venison, pork, flour, onion, garlic salt and pepper. Mix well. Add eggs, one at a time, mixing very well. Add milk and mix thoroughly. Shape into balls, using 3 to 4 tablespoons meat mixture for each ball. Melt butter in skillet and fry balls, turning carefully, adding more butter as needed. Serve with red cabbage. Serves 4.

GROUND MEAT DISHES

•••

THICK N' JUICY MEATBALLS

1/4 cup chopped onion
6 tablespoons butter
1 cup dry breadcrumbs
2 2/3 cups milk
2 eggs, beaten
2 pounds ground venison
1/4 teaspoon parsley flakes
1/4 teaspoon basil
2 teaspoons salt
1/4 teaspoon pepper
2 tablespoons flour

Sauté onion in 2 tablespoons butter in skillet. Soak breadcrumbs in 2/3 cup milk in a mixing bowl. Add eggs, ground venison, parsley, basil, sautéed onion, salt and pepper; and mix well. Form into 1-inch meatballs. Melt remaining 4 tablespoons butter in skillet and cook meatballs until brown. Remove meatballs; set aside. Stir flour into skillet and add remaining 2 cups milk. Cook, stirring constantly, until thickened. Return meatballs to gravy. Simmer 15 minutes and serve hot. Serves 6 to 8.

Casseroles

◆◆◆

A casserole may take some time to fix, but it's worth the effort. Try this Venison Rice Casserole (page 152) and you'll be asking for seconds!

Recipes

CASSEROLES

••

SICILIAN VENISON

2 cups canned green beans
2 pounds ground venison
8 ounces tomato sauce (1 cup)
2 cloves garlic, minced
1/4 teaspoon salt
1/8 teaspoon cinnamon
6 ripe olives, sliced
2 tablespoons ripe olive juice
2 cups ricotta cheese
2 eggs
1/2 cup Parmesan cheese
1/2 teaspoon parsley flakes or 1 teaspoon
fresh parsley, finely chopped

Put green beans in a buttered baking dish. Brown meat in heavy skillet. Add tomato sauce, garlic, salt and cinnamon. Spread meat mixture over the green beans. Combine olives, olive juice, ricotta cheese and eggs. Spread over top of meat mixture. Sprinkle with parmesan cheese. Bake uncovered in 375°F oven about 25 minutes until heated through. Serves 6 to 8.

CASSEROLES

••

ZIPPY PASTA CASSEROLE

1 pound venison, cubed
1 tablespoon shortening
2 cups canned whole tomatoes, cut up
1 carrot, sliced crosswise
1/2 cup celery, chopped
1 onion, chopped
1 teaspoon salt
1 clove garlic, minced
1 teaspoon chili powder
1/4 teaspoon pepper
2 cups water
1 1/2 cups uncooked ziti

Brown meat in shortening. Add undrained tomatoes, carrots, celery, onion, salt, garlic, chili powder and pepper. Cover; simmer for 1 hour. Add water and uncooked ziti. Bring to a boil. Cover and bake in oven 1 hour at 350°F, stirring occasionally. Serves 4.

CASSEROLES

••

MARIA'S SPICY VENISON

1 1/2 pounds ground venison
1 tablespoon cooking oil
1 clove garlic, minced
1/2 teaspoon salt
1/4 medium onion, finely grated
2 tablespoons chili powder
1/2 cup hot salsa sauce
1 dozen small corn tortillas
3/4 cup grated cheddar cheese
3/4 cup chopped ripe olives
1/2 cup water

Brown ground venison in oil in skillet. Season with garlic, salt and onion and cook until meat loses pink color. Add chili powder and salsa sauce and continue cooking 2 minutes. Tear tortillas into bite-sized pieces. In a greased 2-quart casserole, layer meat mixture, tortillas, cheese, and olives, and repeat until all ingredients are used. Top with 1/2-cup water. Cover and bake at 350°F for 30 to 45 minutes. Serves 4 to 6.

CASSEROLES

◆◆

SWISS STYLE VENISON

2 pounds venison round steak
3/4 cup tomato sauce
2 tablespoons cooking oil
1/2 teaspoon salt
1 teaspoon prepared mustard
1/4 teaspoon pepper
4 ounces canned mushroom pieces
1 bay leaf, crushed
1/2 cup diced onion

Place meat in glass casserole. Combine remaining ingredients and pour over meat. Cover casserole with lid or tight-fitting plastic wrap. Refrigerate for at least one hour or overnight if possible. Bake at 350°F for 1 1/2 hours or until venison is tender. Serves 5 to 6.

CASSEROLES

••

MISSISSIPPI-STYLE VENISON

2 tablespoons butter
2 pounds venison, cubed
1 clove garlic, minced
1/2 teaspoon salt
1/8 teaspoon pepper
1 onion, grated
3 1/2 cups canned whole tomatoes
1/8 teaspoon baking soda
1/3 cup heavy cream
2 tablespoons flour
2 tablespoons red wine
2 teaspoons Worcestershire sauce
3 drops angostura bitters (optional)
1 teaspoon parsley flakes
2 tablespoons dry bread crumbs

Melt butter in a heavy skillet and brown meat, gradually adding garlic, salt and pepper as meat cooks. When meat is brown, cover and cook 5 minutes longer, stirring several times. Add onion, cover and cook another 5 minutes. Add tomatoes and baking soda and simmer for 15 minutes. In a small bowl, mix cream and flour until smooth, then add wine, Worcestershire sauce and bitters. Pour cream mixture over meat and tomatoes. Stir until smooth. Cook 5 minutes more and turn into a buttered casserole. Top with parsley flakes and bread crumbs and bake 30 to 40 minutes in a 375°F oven.
Serves 5 to 6.

Casseroles

....

Lima Bean Casserole

2 pounds venison, cubed
1/2 teaspoon onion salt
3 tablespoons cooking oil
3/4 cup water
2 beef bouillon cubes
1 teaspoon salt
1/2 teaspoon ground cardamom
1/4 teaspoon pepper
1 tablespoon lemon juice
8 ounces elbow macaroni
10 ounces lima beans, frozen
3 medium tomatoes, cut into wedges
1 teaspoon sugar
1 tablespoon parsley flakes

Sprinkle meat with onion salt and brown in oil in large skillet. Stir in water, bouillon cubes, salt, cardamom, pepper and lemon juice. Cover; simmer 1 hour or until tender. Cook macaroni according to package directions and place in greased baking dish. Cook lima beans according to label directions and spoon over macaroni to make an edge around baking dish. Spoon meat in the middle and pour cooking liquid over everything. Top with tomato wedges overlapping each other. Sprinkle with sugar and parsley and bake at 350°F for 30 minutes. Serves 6.

CASSEROLES

••

SUNDAY NIGHT SURPRISE

6 large elk or deer steaks
1 cup onion, chopped
1 cup green pepper, chopped
1 - 15 ounce can tomato juice
1 tablespoon Worcestershire Sauce
salt to taste
6 cups sliced raw potatoes

Dredge steaks with flour and brown quickly in hot oil, then remove from pan and set aside. Sauté chopped onion and green pepper. Add steaks back to pan. Stir in tomato juice, Worcestershire sauce, and salt to taste. Simmer two minutes.

Arrange potatoes in a greased Dutch oven or heavy casserole dish. Pour half the sauce over the potatoes. Layer steaks on top of potatoes and top with remaining sauce. Cover and bake in oven at 350°F until meat and potatoes are tender, about 1 to 2 hours. Uncover the last 20 to 30 minutes to thicken sauce.

Note: If you have a penchant for Mexican food, this recipe can be modified by adding 1/4 cup chopped green chilies, 1 to 2 tablespoons chili powder, or Mexican oregano, cumin and cayenne to taste.

This recipe compliments of Suzy Stockton, Stockton Outfitters, Wise River, Montana.

CASSEROLES

••

CARLA'S CASSEROLE

2 pounds venison round steak (1 inch thick)
1/2 cup flour
2 teaspoons salt
1/2 teaspoon pepper
1/8 teaspoon ground oregano
1/2 teaspoon garlic powder
4 tablespoons butter or shortening
4 medium potatoes, diced
2 medium onions, sliced
2 carrots, sliced
1 green pepper, diced
3 cups beef broth
1/4 cup Parmesan cheese

Cut meat into serving-sized pieces. Mix 1/2 cup flour, salt, pepper, oregano and garlic powder. Dredge meat pieces in flour mixture and reserve flour. Brown steaks in butter or shortening. Transfer browned pieces to a 3-quart casserole. Place a layer of vegetables on the meat and sprinkle with the reserved flour mixture. Add the rest of the vegetables and sprinkle the remaining flour mixture on top. Pour broth over casserole, sprinkle cheese on top and cover. Bake at 350°F for 1 hour. Uncover and cook 45 minutes longer or until vegetables and meat are tender. Serves 8.

CASSEROLES

◆◆

ALMOND VENISON DELIGHT

> 1 medium onion, finely chopped
> 1 tablespoon cooking oil
> 1 1/2 pounds ground venison
> 1/4 teaspoon salt
> 1/4 teaspoon garlic salt
> 1/2 teaspoon parsley flakes
> 1 cup sharp cheddar cheese, grated
> 10 3/4 ounce can condensed cream of chicken soup
> 5 ounces condensed cream of mushroom soup
> 2 cups cooked rice
> 4-ounce can button mushrooms, drained
> 1 small finely chopped green pepper
> 1/2 cup shredded cabbage
> 1/2 cup slivered toasted almonds
> 1 teaspoon butter
> 1 cup Chinese crisp noodles

In a skillet sauté onion in oil. Add meat and salt and cook until meat loses pink color. In a large casserole, mix meat with cheese, soups, rice, mushrooms, pepper and cabbage. Place slivered almond in a pie pan with butter or margarine in 350°F oven. When butter has melted, remove pan and stir, so that all the almonds are coated with butter. Return to oven and bake just until edges of nuts show a brownish color. Remove and mix into casserole. Top with Chinese noodles and bake 30 to 40 minutes at 350°F. Serves 6.

CASSEROLES

••

RITA'S EGGPLANT CASSEROLE

1 1/2 pounds ground venison
1 cup chopped onion
1 clove garlic, minced
3 tablespoons olive oil
1 cup Marinara Sauce (recipe below)
1 cup water
3/4 cup dry red wine
1 1/2 teaspoons basil leaf, crumbled
1/2 teaspoon oregano leaf, crumbled
1 medium eggplant, peeled and sliced (about 1 pound)
1/2 cup olive oil
1/2 cup grated Parmesan cheese
1 pound mozzarella cheese, thickly sliced

Brown venison with onion and garlic in 3 tablespoons olive oil in a large skillet. Add Marinara Sauce, water, wine, basil and oregano. Cover and simmer 20 minutes. Sauté half the eggplant slices in 1/4 cup of olive oil until limp and golden. Add remaining oil and sauté remaining eggplant. When all the eggplant is browned, place in a shallow baking dish. Spoon meat sauce over eggplant. Sprinkle Parmesan cheese evenly over casserole. Top with sliced mozzarella. Bake at 350°F for 20 to 30 minutes. Serves 6.

Marinara Sauce

4 tablespoons olive oil
6 cups tomato juice
1/2 teaspoon basil

3 cloves garlic, sliced very thin
4 cups tomato sauce
1/2 teaspoon oregano

Brown garlic slices in olive oil until very brown. Reduce heat and remove garlic from the oil. When oil has cooled enough to prevent spattering, add tomato juice and sauce to oil. Return to a moderate heat, and add oregano and basil. Simmer 2 1/2 hours, stirring occasionally. Yields about 1 quart.

CASSEROLES

••

GROUND VENISON IN CABBAGE LEAVES

12 large outside cabbage leaves
1 pound ground venison
1/4 cup grated onion
2 tablespoons chopped parsley
3/4 teaspoon salt
1/2 teaspoon thyme
1 clove garlic, mashed
1/8 teaspoon cayenne pepper
1/4 teaspoon paprika
3/4 cup cooked rice
Butter or margarine
1 cup tomato juice

Wash and cook cabbage leaves 3 to 5 minutes in boiling water. Drain and set aside. Mix meat, onions, parsley, salt, thyme, garlic, cayenne pepper, and paprika. Mix in cooked rice. Place a portion of meat-rice mixture on each cabbage leaf. Fold in ends and roll up. Tie or secure each roll with a toothpick. Place in greased baking dish. Dot each with butter or margarine. Pour tomato juice over rolls and bake at 350°F for 1 hour. Serves 10.

CASSEROLES

◆◆

VENISON RICE CASSEROLE

1 pound ground venison
1/4 cup diced onion
1/4 cup finely chopped green pepper
1/2 cup dry breadcrumbs
1/2 cup tomato sauce
1/2 teaspoon salt
1/4 teaspoon pepper
1/8 teaspoon ground oregano
Rice Topping Recipe (given below)

Preheat oven to 350°F. In a large bowl thoroughly combine above ingredients. Pat mixture into the bottom and sides of a greased 9-inch pie pan. Place in oven and bake 15 minutes while preparing Rice Topping recipe below.

Rice Topping

2 cups cooked rice
1/4 cup water
1/4 teaspoon salt
3/4 cup tomato sauce
1 cup sharp cheddar cheese, grated

Combine rice, water, salt, tomato sauce and 1/2 cup of the cheese. Pour over partially baked meat mixture. Cover tightly with foil and bake for 15 minutes. Remove foil and sprinkle with remaining cheese. Bake uncovered 15 to 20 minutes longer. Cut into wedges. Serves 4 to 6.

CASSEROLES

•••

ELK BURGER CASSEROLE

    1 pound ground meat
    2 cups cooked rice
    1 can corn, with juice
    1 can cream of chicken soup
    2 to 3 dashes liquid smoke
    3 tablespoons barbecue sauce

Brown meat in small amount of oil until it loses its pink color. Place all remaining ingredients in casserole and mix, add meat. Bake at 350°F for 30 minutes or until heated through.

EASY STEAK & RICE CASSEROLE

    1 1/2 pounds venison round steak (3/4 inch thick)
    1 cup uncooked rice
    2 cups water
    1 envelope dry onion soup
    10 3/4 ounces canned condensed cream of celery soup
    1 teaspoon salt
    1/8 teaspoon pepper

Cut steak into serving-sized pieces and place in a casserole. Mix together remaining ingredients and pour over meat. Cover and bake at 400°F for 1 1/2 hours or until steak is tender. Serves 6.

CASSEROLES

••

ORIENTAL CASSEROLE

   1 pound ground venison
   1 to 2 tablespoons cooking oil
   1 cup cooked rice
   1/2 cup diced celery
   2 medium onions, chopped
   1/4 cup soy sauce
   1/4 teaspoon pepper
   10 3/4 ounce can condensed cream of chicken soup
   10 3/4 ounce can condensed cream of mushroom soup
   2 cups water
   1 cup bean sprouts
   1 1/2 cups Chinese noodles

In a large skillet, brown meat lightly in oil. Put cooked meat and next eight ingredients in a large baking dish. Mix, cover and bake 45 minutes at 350°F. Add bean sprouts on top and return dish to oven to bake for another 20 minutes. Sprinkle Chinese noodles over the top of casserole and bake for 15 minutes longer. Serves 4.

CASSEROLES

•••

VENISON NOODLE BAKE

3 tablespoons cooking oil
1 onion, chopped
1/4 teaspoon dried red pepper, crumbled
1/4 cup green pepper, diced
2 pounds ground venison
1/2 teaspoon salt
2 cups canned whole tomatoes, undrained
1 cup whole kernel corn
1/3 cup sliced pimento-stuffed green olives
3/4 cup grated American cheese
1 pound egg noodles, cooked and drained

Heat oil in skillet and sauté onions with red and green peppers until onions are translucent. Remove onions and peppers and set aside. Add ground venison and salt to skillet, and cook until meat loses its pink color. (Additional oil may be necessary to prevent meat from sticking if the fat content of meat is low.) When meat begins to brown, add cooked onions and peppers, and tomatoes and simmer 5 to 10 minutes. Add corn and half of the green olives; simmer an additional 5 minutes. Stir in drained noodles which have been cooked according to package directions. Pour all into a large casserole dish. Sprinkle top with cheese and remaining olives. Bake uncovered for 45 minutes to an hour at 350°F. Serves 8.

SPECIALTY DISHES

◆◆◆

Recipes

Specialty Dishes

◆◆◆

You'll impress your dinner guests when you cook up one of the tasty recipes in this chapter. The Artichoke Elk recipe pictured here will work on most cuts of game.

Artichoke Elk

2 pounds elk steak
Milk to cover steaks
Flour to coat steaks
1/2 teaspoon salt
1/2 teaspoon pepper
1/4 teaspoon garlic salt
4 tablespoons vegetable oil
1 lemon
1 cup white wine
1/2 cup marinated artichoke hearts, chopped

Cut elk steaks into serving sized pieces. Pound each filet until it is about twice its original size. Place meat in shallow bowl, and add enough milk just to cover steaks. Soak steaks in milk for 15 minutes. Drain milk and dredge meat in mixture of flour, salt, pepper, and garlic salt. Heat oil in skillet, add steaks and cook on one side until brown. After turning steaks to cook the other side, squeeze the juice of one lemon over the meat as it continues to cook another couple of minutes. Add the white wine, cover and simmer another 2 to 4 minutes. Add the artichoke hearts, cover and simmer another 1 to 2 minutes until artichokes are heated through. Serve at once. Serves 6.

This recipe compliments of Kathy Etling, St. Louis, Missouri.

SPECIALTY DISHES

◆◆

KALBI VENISON

1 1/2 pounds venison loin steaks, cut into 1/2-inch pieces
6 slices of ginger root approximately 1/8 inch thick
4 large cloves garlic
1/2 cup onion, chopped
1/2 to 3/4 cup soy sauce
3 tablespoons sugar
1/2 cup chopped green onion tops
2 teaspoons sesame seeds

Place the ginger root, garlic, onion, soy sauce and sugar in a blender and blend until smooth (about 30 seconds). Taste marinade and add additional soy sauce to mellow the flavor if desired.

Place venison in a glass casserole dish and pour the marinade over the venison. Sprinkle sesame seed and green onions on top. Cover with plastic wrap. For best results, marinate over night. Grill venison based on preference of well, medium or rare. This is a Korean dish. Serves 4.

SPECIALTY DISHES

••

ORIENTAL PEPPER STEAK

1 pound venison steak, cut in thin strips
3 tablespoons olive oil
1 clove garlic, minced
1/2 teaspoon ginger
2 green peppers, sliced thin
2 tomatoes, peeled and quartered
1 cup bean sprouts
3 tablespoons cornstarch
1/4 cup sherry, vermouth or water
1 teaspoon sugar
3 tablespoons soy sauce
Salt
Pepper
3 scallions, thinly sliced

Slice steak across the grain as thinly as possible. In a skillet, brown strips in oil, garlic, salt and ginger over moderate heat for 10 to 15 minutes. Add green peppers. Cover and cook over low heat for 5 minutes. Add the tomatoes and bean sprouts, cover and simmer a few minutes longer. In a bowl, mix cornstarch with either sherry, vermouth or water, and the sugar. Season mixture with salt, pepper and soy sauce. Pour mixture over meat in skillet and bring to a boil slowly, stirring constantly. When cornstarch has thickened, add the scallions and cook 1 minute longer before serving. Serves 4.

SPECIALTY DISHES

••

STEAK 'N ONION RINGS

1 pound venison steak
1/2 teaspoon instant meat tenderizer
2 tablespoons cornstarch
4 tablespoons sherry
1/2 teaspoon soy sauce
1/2 teaspoon Teriyaki sauce
4 to 6 large onions, sliced
2 to 4 tablespoons cooking oil

Cut meat into strips 1/4 inch wide and 2 to 4 inches long and place in a bowl. Add tenderizer, cornstarch, sherry, soy sauce, Teriyaki sauce. Sprinkle with salt. Mix and let stand at least 15 minutes. Separate onion slices into rings and fry in hot oil in a heavy skillet or wok over medium heat for 2 to 4 minutes, stirring constantly. They should still be somewhat crisp. Remove to heated platter. Place steak strips in hot skillet, adding more oil if necessary and stir constantly for 2 to 4 minutes. Put onions back into skillet and mix with meat. Serve at once, with rice. Serves 3 to 4.

SPECIALTY DISHES

◆◆◆

SOUTH PACIFIC VENISON

1 pound venison steak
1/4 cup flour
1/4 cup butter or margarine
1/2 cup boiling water
1/4 teaspoon leaf basil
1/2 teaspoon rosemary
1 teaspoon salt
1/8 teaspoon pepper
2 to 3 green peppers, diced
3/4 cup pineapple chunks, drained

Cut steak into cubes. Dredge in flour and brown in Dutch oven in butter or margarine. Add water, basil, rosemary, salt and pepper and simmer, covered, until tender, about 1 to 1 1/2 hours. Add green pepper and pineapple chunks and simmer 5 minutes. Meanwhile prepare sauce recipe below. Pour sauce over meat and bring everything to a boil, stirring constantly. Reduce heat and simmer 5 minutes. Serve over Chinese noodles or cooked rice. Serves 4 to 6.

Sauce

2 1/2 teaspoons cornstarch
1/4 cup vinegar
1/2 cup pineapple juice
1/2 cup sugar
2 1/2 teaspoons soy sauce

In a saucepan, blend the cornstarch, vinegar, pineapple juice, sugar and soy sauce until smooth. Bring mixture to a boil, and cook, stirring constantly, until sauce is thick and transparent.

SPECIALTY DISHES

••

SWEET & SOUR ANTELOPE

   1 pound antelope round steak, cut into thin strips
   1 3/4 cups water
   1 teaspoon salt
   1/4 cup soy sauce
   1 clove garlic, whole
   1/3 cup sugar
   1/4 teaspoon ground ginger
   1/4 cup cornstarch
   1/4 cup cider vinegar
   1/3 cup pineapple juice
   3/4 cup pineapple chunks
   1 green pepper, cut into chunks

Place antelope, water, salt, soy sauce and garlic in a two quart sauce pan. Cook on HIGH until at a boil, about 5 minutes. Cover, reduce heat and simmer until meat is barely cooked, about 12-15 minutes. Remove meat and set aside. Discard garlic. Strain broth through cheesecloth (or coffee filter) to remove meat drippings; reserve broth.

In a saucepan, blend the sugar, cornstarch, vinegar, pineapple juice, and ginger until smooth. Gradually stir in meat broth, and mix well. Cook on HIGH until sauce is thick and transparent; stirring thoroughly about every two minutes until done, about 6-8 minutes.

Combine sauce with antelope meat, add pineapple and green pepper. Allow mixture to sit a few minutes before serving over rice.

This recipe compliments of Janette Zumbo, West Jordan, Utah.

SPECIALTY DISHES

CURRIED BIGHORN SHEEP

1 pound sheep loin, cut into 1-inch cubes
2 to 3 tablespoons flour
1/4 cup onion, finely chopped
1/2 to 1 teaspoon curry powder (to taste)
1/4 teaspoon ground ginger
1/2 teaspoon salt
dash of pepper
1/2 cup chicken stock
1/2 teaspoon lemon juice

Brown the meat in hot oil in a large skillet. When browned on all sides, remove the meat from the pan. Add flour to pan drippings, and stir well until flour is cooked, about 3 minutes. Add remaining ingredients except lemon juice, and bring slowly to a boil. Return the meat to the pan and reduce heat to simmer. Add dash of lemon juice, and cook until meat is tender.

SPECIALTY DISHES

◆◆

CURRIED VENISON STEAK

　　2 to 4 tablespoons cooking oil
　　1 onion, sliced
　　1 clove garlic, sliced very thin
　　1 tablespoon curry powder
　　1 pound venison steak, in 1-inch cubes
　　1/2 teaspoon salt
　　1/2 cup tomato paste
　　1 cup beef broth
　　1 lime or lemon

Heat oil in skillet, add onions and garlic and cook until brown. Add curry powder; stir and continue to fry 2 to 3 minutes. Add the meat and cook on all sides. Stir in tomato paste and broth. Cover and simmer for 1 1/2 hours, or until meat is tender and gravy thick. Add the juice from the lime or lemon. Serve over rice. Serves 4.

SPECIALTY DISHES

●●

PARMESAN MEDALLIONS

1 1/2 pounds venison round steak (1/4 to 1/2 inch thick)
1/2 cup dry breadcrumbs
1/2 teaspoon leaf oregano
1/4 teaspoon basil
1/2 teaspoon garlic salt
1/2 teaspoon salt
1 egg
2 tablespoons milk
4 to 5 tablespoons olive oil
2 cups Marinara Sauce
1/2 pound mozzarella cheese, thinly sliced
Parmesan cheese

Cut meat into small, serving-sized pieces. Pound steaks with meat mallet until thin and flat, about three inches in diameter. In small bowl, mix together breadcrumbs, oregano, basil, garlic salt and salt. Beat together egg and milk with fork in another bowl. Dip each piece of meat in egg and then in breadcrumb mixture until well coated with crumbs. Place pieces on waxed paper for 10 to 15 minutes; then fry in olive oil until golden brown. Spread 2 or 3 tablespoons Marinara sauce in the bottom of a shallow baking dish to prevent sticking. Arrange steaks in the dish and cover each piece of meat with mozzarella cheese. Top with remaining sauce and sprinkle with Parmesan cheese. Cover and bake 1 hour in 325°F oven or until meat is very tender. Serves 5 to 6.

SPECIALTY DISHES

••

QUICK VENISON LASAGNA

1 pound ground venison
1 tablespoon cooking oil
1 small onion, chopped
1/2 pound smoked link sausage, cut into 1/2-inch chunks
16 ounces tomato sauce (2 cups)
1 cup water
1/2 teaspoon salt
1/2 teaspoon leaf basil
1/2 teaspoon parsley flakes
1/2 teaspoon leaf oregano
1 pound lasagna noodles
1 egg, beaten
1 cup ricotta or cottage cheese
1/4 cup canned, sliced ripe olives
1/2 pound mozzarella cheese, thinly sliced

In a heavy skillet, brown venison with onion in hot oil. Stir in sausage, tomato sauce, water, salt, basil, parsley, and oregano. Simmer uncovered 20 minutes. Meanwhile, cook noodles according to package directions. Drain. Combine egg, ricotta (or cottage) cheese and olives. Place a small amount of sauce in the bottom of a 9 X 13 inch baking dish. Then layer half of the noodles, half of the ricotta mixture, half of the mozzarella slices and half of the meat sauce. Repeat layers, using the rest of the ingredients. Bake at 375°F for 30 minutes. Let stand 10 minutes before serving. Serves 5 to 6.

SPECIALTY DISHES

••

MEATBALLS NAPOLITANO

4 tablespoons olive oil
3 cloves garlic, thinly sliced
46 ounces canned tomato juice (5 3/4 cups)
28 ounces canned tomato sauce (3 1/2 cups)
1/2 teaspoon leaf oregano
1/4 teaspoon leaf basil
1/2 teaspoon garlic salt
1 pound ground venison
1/2 cup dry breadcrumbs (unseasoned)
1 egg
1/3 teaspoon leaf oregano
2 tablespoons Parmesan cheese
1/3 teaspoon parsley flakes
1/3 teaspoon garlic salt
1 tablespoon cooking oil

In Dutch oven, brown garlic slices in olive oil until very brown. Remove from heat, discard garlic and let oil cool. Add tomato juice, tomato sauce, oregano, basil and garlic salt to oil. Bring to a boil, reduce heat, and simmer for 2 1/2 hours with lid slightly ajar to prevent splattering. Stir occasionally. Meanwhile, thoroughly mix ground venison, breadcrumbs, egg, oregano, Parmesan cheese, parsley flakes and garlic salt. Form into balls and brown in oil in a large skillet, turning frequently until balls are cooked completely through. Add the meatballs to the sauce and simmer together for a least 30 minutes more. Serve with any kind of pasta, topped with more Parmesan cheese. Serves 4 to 6.

SPECIALTY DISHES

●●●

VENISON CREPES WITH HAM

    1 pound ground venison
    1/4 teaspoon salt
    1/8 teaspoon pepper
    1 medium onion, chopped
    1 tablespoon cooking oil
    1 1/2 cups chopped ham
    1/4 cup flour
    1 cup beef bouillon
    1/4 cup sliced, canned mushrooms
    1 tablespoon butter
    1 tablespoon flour
    1 cup milk
    1 tablespoon Parmesan cheese
    3 tablespoons grated Swiss cheese
    1/2 teaspoon prepared mustard

Brown venison and onions in oil; season with salt and pepper. Add ham and flour and stir. Add beef bouillon and mushrooms and simmer for 30 minutes. In a saucepan melt butter and add 1 tablespoon flour, stirring with wire whisk. Add 1 cup milk, stirring constantly over moderate heat until sauce is thickened. Add cheeses and mustard. Fill 12 to 16 crepes with meat mixture, roll up and place in baking dish. Pour sauce over top and bake for 25 minutes at 375°F. Serves 8.

Crepe Batter

    8 eggs   1/2 teaspoon salt
    4 cups flour   4-1/2 cups milk
    1/2 cup melted butter or oil

Combine all ingredients in a blender and blend one minute. Scrape sides of blender and mix another 15 seconds or until smooth. Refrigerate at least one hour, and then cook in crepe pan and store until ready to use.

SPECIALTY DISHES

◆◆

VENISON KABOBS CARBONADE

Marinade

> **12 ounces beer**
> **1/3 cup diced onion**
> **2 tablespoons cooking oil**
> **3/4 teaspoon salt**
> **1 teaspoon curry powder**
> **1/2 teaspoon ground ginger**
> **1/4 teaspoon garlic powder**

In a glass bowl, combine beer, onion, oil, salt, curry powder, ginger and garlic powder.

> **1 1/2 to 2 pounds venison steak, cubed**
> **1/2 pound large fresh mushrooms**
> **2 large green peppers, cut into chunks**

Place meat in shallow glass dish. Pour marinade over meat, and refrigerate for 4 to 5 hours. Drain meat, reserving the marinade. Skewer meat, alternating with mushrooms and peppers. Broil or grill over coals, brushing with marinade frequently. Serve immediately. Serves 4 to 6.

SPECIALTY DISHES

◆◆◆

CREPES WITH VENISON SLIVERS

3 to 3 1/2 pound venison roast
1/4 teaspoon garlic salt
1/2 teaspoon salt
1/8 teaspoon pepper
1/8 teaspoon oregano
1 package (1 1/2 ounces) dry onion soup mix
10 3/4 ounces condensed cream of mushroom soup
1 cup dry red wine
1 cup flour
4 ounces canned, sliced mushrooms (1/2 cup) or
1 cup sliced fresh mushrooms
10 to 15 cooked crepes

Sprinkle roast with salt, pepper, garlic salt, and oregano. Place in Dutch oven and add dry onion soup mix, undiluted mushroom soup, wine and 1 cup water. Cover and simmer 4 to 4 1/2 hours or until meat is tender. Remove meat. Dissolve flour in small amount of water and gradually stir into boiling meat broth, stirring constantly. Stir in mushrooms and remove from heat when sauce is thickened. Meanwhile slice meat thinly into pieces about 1/2 X 2 inches. Place 3 or 4 tablespoons meat slices on each cooked crepe and top with 1 tablespoon sauce. Place in shallow baking dish. Pour remaining sauce over filled crepes. Cover and bake 20 minutes at 350°F. Makes 10 to 15 crepes. (Crepe Recipe given with preceding, Crepes With Ham Recipe.)

SPECIALTY DISHES

◆◆

FRENCH STYLE VENISON KABOBS

1 to 2 pounds venison steak (any cut) cubed
Bottle French dressing
Mushrooms (fresh, stemmed)
Cherry Tomatoes
Green peppers, sliced
Water chestnuts
Small onion chunks

Place cubed venison in a bowl. Pour enough French dressing over meat to coat well. Marinate for 1 hour or more. Skewer meat, mushrooms, pineapple, peppers, water chestnuts and onions on skewers according to individual taste. Grill over charcoal, basting lightly with dressing.

◆◆

SOUTH OF THE BORDER VENISON STEAK

Marinade

1/2 cup tequila
3 tablespoons lime juice
2 tablespoons olive oil
1 teaspoon freshly grated orange peel
1 small dried red pepper, crushed

2 to 3 pound venison round steak, 2 inches thick
2 tablespoons coarse salt

Trim fat from meat. Rub salt into meat and place in a shallow dish. Combine tequila, lime juice, olive oil, orange peel and pepper. Pour over meat and refrigerate 6 to 8 hours, turning every few hours. Grill meat until done over charcoal coals, basting with marinade several times.

Specialty Dishes

••

Northwest Enchiladas

2 pounds ground venison
1 medium onion, chopped
2 cans (15 ounces each) tomato sauce
1/4 to 1/2 pound cheddar cheese, grated
1 tablespoon chili powder
salt and pepper to taste
12 taco shells (soft)
oil

Brown ground meat and onion in small amount of oil; season to taste with salt and pepper. In bowl, season tomato sauce with chili powder. In small skillet, heat taco shells in oil individually, and drain on paper towels. After heating 2 to 3 shells, fill drained shells with ground meat, about 2 table-spoons seasoned tomato sauce, and grated cheese (to taste). Roll taco shells and lay loose ends down in a 9" x 13" baking pan. When all the taco shells are filled, cover with remaining tomato sauce, and top with grated cheese. Bake in preheated oven at 350°F for about 30 minutes. Serves 3-4.

This recipe compliments of Bruce and Elaine Koffler, Koffler Boats, Junction City, Oregon.

SPECIALTY DISHES

$\blacklozenge$

JOSE'S SENSATIONAL VENISON

2 to 2 1/2 pound venison round steak
1/2 teaspoon salt
1/8 teaspoon garlic salt
1/4 teaspoon onion salt
1/8 teaspoon pepper
15 ounces canned tamales in sauce
1 teaspoon instant beef bouillon granules
1/2 cup boiling water
8 ounces tomato sauce
1/2 to 1 teaspoon hot salsa sauce
1/2 cup Monterey jack or Swiss cheese, grated

Pound meat with a meat mallet on both sides. Sprinkle with salt, garlic salt, onion salt and pepper. Unwrap tamales and place in bowl, breaking them up slightly with a fork. Spread over steaks. Roll steak up — jelly-roll style. Tie closed with thread. Place in a shallow baking dish. In a saucepan dissolve bouillon in boiling water. Stir in tomato sauce and hot sauce. Pour over meat. Bake uncovered at 350°F for 1 1/2 to 2 hours, or until meat is tender, basting with sauce often. Remove string and cut into serving-sized pieces. Top meat with cheese and serve hot. Serves 8.

SPECIALTY DISHES

◆◆◆

SONORAN MEAT PIE

1 to 1 1/2 pounds ground venison
1 onion, diced
4 ounces diced green chilies (1/2 cup)
1 teaspoon chili powder
1/4 teaspoon garlic salt or 1 clove garlic, minced
1/2 teaspoon salt
1/8 teaspoon pepper
3 tablespoons ketchup
2 tablespoons salsa sauce
4 eggs
2 cups milk
1 cup biscuit mix
3/4 cup grated cheddar cheese
1/2 cup grated jack cheese

Preheat oven to 375°F. Brown meat with onion, chilies, chili powder, garlic salt, salt and pepper. Stir ketchup and salsa sauce into meat mixture. Blend eggs, milk and biscuit mix in blender. Place meat mixture in buttered baking dish. Reserve 2 tablespoons of jack cheese and 2 tablespoons of cheddar cheese. Sprinkle the rest of the cheeses on the meat. Pour the biscuit mix on meat and cheese. Top with reserved cheese. Bake 35 to 40 minutes. Serves 4 to 6.

SPECIALTY DISHES

••

HOBO FAJITAS

Marinade

12 ounces beer
1 cup Italian oil-and-vinegar salad dressing

Combine beer and salad dressing for marinade.

2 pounds thin, round venison steak
Sour cream
Grated cheese
Hot taco sauce or salsa sauce
12 flour tortillas

Pierce meat with fork and place in shallow baking dish. Pour on marinade, cover, and let set overnight. Grill steak, or bake in moderate oven for 45 minutes or until well done. With either method of cooking steak, baste periodically with marinade during cooking. Slice meat into thin strips. Heat tortillas in microwave, oven or bun warmer. Layer thinly sliced steak, sour cream, grated cheese and hot sauce on hot flour tortillas and roll up. Makes 12.

SPECIALTY DISHES

••

CHIMICHANGAS

    2 pounds venison chunks
    1 1/2 cups water
    2 cloves garlic, minced
    2 tablespoons chili powder
    2 tablespoons vinegar
    2 teaspoons crushed leaf oregano
    1/4 teaspoon basil
    1 teaspoon salt
    1 teaspoon ground cumin
    1/2 teaspoon pepper
    1 dozen large flour tortillas
    Cooking oil
    2 cups shredded lettuce
    2 cups guacamole

In saucepan, combine meat, water, garlic, chili powder, vinegar, oregano, basil, salt, cumin and pepper. Bring to a boil. Cover; reduce heat and simmer 2 hours or until meat is very tender. Uncover and simmer 15 minutes longer or until almost all of the water has evaporated. Remove from heat and shred meat, using two forks. Heat tortillas. Spoon 1/4-cup meat mixture onto each tortilla near edge. Fold edge nearest filling, up and over filling, covering the mixture. Fold up the two sides envelope fashion and roll up. Fasten with toothpicks. In skillet fry filled tortillas in hot oil until tortillas are golden brown. Drain on paper towels. Keep warm and top with lettuce and guacamole. Makes 12.

SPECIALTY DISHES

••

MUY GRANDE ENCHILADAS

2 pounds ground venison
1/2 teaspoon garlic salt
1/2 small onion, chopped
10 3/4 ounces condensed cream of chicken soup
1/2 cup sour cream
2 ounces canned green chilies
1 cup grated cheddar cheese
1/3 cup taco or salsa sauce
2 tablespoons grated cheddar cheese
1 dozen corn tortillas
1/2 cup cooking oil
1/2 soup can of water (5 ounces)

Brown ground meat with garlic salt and onions. Remove from heat. Mix soup, sour cream, chilies, one cup cheese and taco sauce into meat mixture. Fry tortillas in hot oil briefly on both sides in skillet. Drain excess oil onto paper towels as you remove them from skillet. Fill each tortilla with meat mixture and place in shallow baking dish. Top with remaining meat mixture. Add water carefully to the sides of the dish. Top with the remaining two tablespoons of cheese. Bake at 350°F for 30 minutes. Makes 12 enchiladas.

SPECIALTY DISHES

●●●

SANTE FE STROGANOFF

1 1/2 pounds venison, cubed
Flour, salt, pepper
2 tablespoons shortening
1 small onion, chopped
1/2 teaspoon garlic salt
4 ounces canned mushrooms, reserving 1/2 cup of liquid
10 1/2 ounces canned condensed tomato soup
1 tablespoon Worcestershire sauce
6 to 8 drops Tabasco sauce
1/2 teaspoon crushed chili pepper
1/2 teaspoon salt
1/8 teaspoon pepper
1 cup sour cream
1 tablespoon Parmesan cheese

Dredge meat in flour seasoned to taste with salt and pepper. Melt shortening in pressure cooker and brown meat well. Remove cooker from heat. Add onions, garlic salt, mushrooms and liquid, tomato soup, Worcestershire sauce, Tobasco sauce, chili pepper, salt and pepper. Mix well. Close cover securely. Follow manufacturers directions when cooking. Immediately cool cooker. Add sour cream and heat (do not boil) for 10 minutes in uncovered cooker. Sprinkle with Parmesan cheese and serve over wide noodles. Serves 6.

SPECIALTY DISHES

••

VENISON BAKED IN BEER

> **3 pounds venison, cubed**
> **1/4 cup flour**
> **1/2 teaspoon salt**
> **1/4 teaspoon pepper**
> **2 medium onions, diced**
> **3-4 tablespoons cooking oil**
> **4 cubes beef bouillon dissolved in 4 cups hot water**
> **2 tablespoons ketchup**
> **2 cups beer**
> **1 clove garlic, peeled**
> **1 bay leaf**
> **2 cloves**
> **1/4 teaspoon thyme**
> **1/2 teaspoon salt**
> **1/4 teaspoon pepper**
> **2 carrots, sliced crosswise**
> **2 potatoes, cubed**

Mix flour, salt and pepper and dredge meat in mixture. Brown meat and onions in oil in Dutch oven, then add bouillon, ketchup, and beer. Put garlic, bay leaf, cloves and thyme in herb bag and add to pot. Cover and simmer for 2 hours. Add salt, pepper, carrots and potatoes and simmer covered about 45 minutes or until meat and vegetables are tender. Remove herb bag and serve. Serves 6 to 8.

SPECIALTY DISHES

••

ZESTY VENISON BURGUNDY

3 tablespoons vegetable oil
2 pounds venison, cut in 1-inch cubes
2 tablespoons flour
1 1/2 cups chicken broth
3/4 teaspoon salt
1 clove garlic, minced
2 large onions, sliced
1/2 teaspoon basil
Grated peel of half of lemon
2 teaspoons paprika
1 cup burgundy
1/2 pound raw mushrooms, chopped
2 teaspoons parsley, finely chopped

Melt shortening in Dutch oven and brown meat lightly. Sprinkle flour over meat and mix well. Add chicken broth, salt, garlic, onions, basil, lemon peel and paprika. Cover and simmer for 30 minutes. Add wine and simmer for 1 hour (add additional chicken broth if liquid is low). Add mushrooms and parsley, cover and simmer 15 minutes or until venison is tender. Serves 5.

SPECIALTY DISHES

◆◆◆

VENISON HEART LIKE YOU'VE NEVER HAD IT BEFORE

1 venison heart
2 tablespoons cooking oil
1 1/2 cups water
2/3 cup uncooked rice
1/3 cup chopped celery
1/4 cup chopped green pepper
2 ounces canned mushrooms, sliced
10 3/4 ounces condensed cream of mushroom soup
2 tablespoons dry onion soup mix
1/4 teaspoon garlic salt
1/4 teaspoon parsley flakes

Rinse heart and remove outer membrane. Cut the heart open and cube tender fleshy parts of the heart, discarding gristle and venous hard parts and any fat. Brown cubes in cooking oil. Add water and simmer 45 minutes. Add uncooked rice, celery, and green pepper; bring to a boil. Reduce heat; cover and simmer until rice is tender (about 20 minutes). Drain mushrooms; stir into heart mixture with mushroom and onion soups, salt and parsley flakes. Simmer 10 minutes more. Serves 6.

SPECIALTY DISHES

◆◆

LOLITA'S VENISON LIVER

6 slices bacon
2/3 cup chopped onion
2 cloves garlic, minced
1/4 cup flour
1 1/4 teaspoons chili powder
3/4 teaspoon salt
2 ounces canned chopped green chilies
1 1/2 pounds venison liver
16 ounces or 2 cups canned whole tomatoes, cut up
12 ounces or 1 1/2 cups canned whole kernel corn, drained
12 flour tortillas

In skillet, cook bacon until crisp. Remove bacon; crumble and set aside. Cook onion and garlic in bacon fat until onion is transparent. Combine flour, chili powder and salt. Cut liver into thin strips and dredge in flour mixture. Add liver to onion in skillet and brown quickly on all sides. Stir in crumbled bacon, undrained tomatoes, chilies and corn. Simmer covered for 15 minutes. Serve with tortillas. Serves 6.

SPECIALTY DISHES

◆◆◆

VENISON LIVER AND BACON

2 pounds deer liver, sliced 1/4-inch thick
Milk
1/2 cup flour
3/4 teaspoon salt
1 teaspoon finely minced fresh parsley
1/2 teaspoon pepper
1/2 cup margarine
1 tablespoon soy sauce
8 slices bacon

Refrigerate liver slices overnight in milk. Drain. Pat dry and dredge slices in mixture of flour, salt, pepper and parsley. Sauté liver slices in margarine over high heat until lightly brown, adding soy sauce as venison begins cooking. Cook about five minutes on each side. In another skillet fry bacon slices until crisp. Drain bacon and serve on top of liver slices. Serves 3 to 4.

SPECIALTY DISHES

••

ZUMBO'S FAVORITE BARBECUED VENISON RIBS

Super Marinade Sauce

> 1 tablespoon Worcestershire sauce
> 1/8 teaspoon Tabasco sauce
> 1 cup ketchup
> 1 cup water
> 1/4 cup vinegar
> 1 tablespoon sugar
> 1 teaspoon salt
> 1 teaspoon sesame seed
> 1 teaspoon celery seed

Combine all ingredients and marinate ribs for 8 to 10 hours (or overnight) in refrigerator. Cook ribs as shown below, and be sure to reserve marinade to brush on ribs during cooking.

> 4 pounds venison ribs
> 1 to 2 teaspoons salt (or to taste)
> Barbeque Grill (Weber Smoker preferred)

Marinate ribs as directed above. Remove ribs from marinade and reserve sauce. Sprinkle 2 teaspoons salt evenly over ribs. Start charcoal in Weber barbecue/smoker. When coals are burning well cover them completely with hickory chips that have been soaked in water for about 30 minutes. Place ribs, bone side down, on grill of smoker, away from coals. Close hood on smoker and cook slowly for 3 1/2 to 4 hours, basting with Super Marinade Sauce frequently. Serves 4 to 5.

SPECIALTY DISHES

••

BAKED SWEET & SOUR GAME RIBS

3 pounds venison ribs
1/2 cup flour
2 to 3 onions, sliced
1/2 cup hot water
5 cloves garlic, pressed into pulp
2 large bay leaves
1/3 cup ketchup
1/4 cup tarragon vinegar
1/2 cup (heaping) dark brown sugar

Mix flour with seasoned salt and pepper. Coat ribs in flour mixture. Brown ribs in oil in Dutch oven. Remove ribs and add onions to oil. Sauté until limp. Return ribs to Dutch oven, placing them on the onions. Mix remaining ingredients, and pour the sweet and sour mixture over the ribs. Cover and bake at 350°F for 2-1/2 hours or until tender.

SPECIALTY DISHES

••

CROSWELL'S RIBS

    3 pounds ribs
    1/2 clove garlic, minced
    2 diced onions
    2 tablespoons butter
    1-1/2 cups canned tomatoes
    1-1/2 cups celery, diced
    1-1/2 cups ketchup
    2-1/2 tablespoons brown sugar
    4 dashes Tabasco
    3/4 teaspoon dry mustard
    3 cups beef bouillon
    salt, pepper

Rub ribs with garlic clove and place in crock pot. Add enough water or chicken broth to cover ribs and cook slowly for 4 to 5 hours until meat falls off bone.

In pan, cook onions in butter until translucent. Add all remaining ingredients except ribs and garlic and simmer one hour.

Place ribs in baking pan and cover with sauce. Place lid on pan and bake covered for 45 minutes in preheated oven at 325°F. Reserve some sauce for serving at table.

This recipe compliments of Delores Croswell, Washougal, Washington.

SPECIALTY DISHES

◆◆

MARINATED RIBS

   4 pounds venison ribs
   1/2 cup soy sauce
   1/3 cup sugar
   2 tablespoons vinegar
   1 tablespoon vegetable oil
   1 teaspoon ginger
   3/4 teaspoon lemon-pepper
   1/4 teaspoon garlic salt
   1 medium onion, diced
   1 medium green pepper, diced
   1/4 cup butter
   2 1/2 cups water

Put meat in large glass bowl. Prepare marinade by combining soy sauce, sugar, vinegar, oil, ginger, lemon-pepper, and garlic salt. Pour over meat, cover and refrigerate several hours, turning occasionally. When ribs are ready to cook, sauté onion and green pepper in butter, then remove and set aside. Brown the ribs in a skillet for about 10 minutes. Put ribs in a large casserole dish, and add onion, green pepper, marinade, water, and additional fat if meat is very lean. Cover and bake in oven at 325°F for 1-1/2 hours. Remove lid and bake an additional 30 minutes or until meat is tender.

◆◆◆

FINGER LICKIN' VENISON RIBS

**3 to 4 pounds venison ribs, individually cut
3 tablespoons cooking oil
1 teaspoon salt
1/8 teaspoon garlic salt
1/8 teaspoon pepper
3 medium onions, sliced
3/4 cup water
2 tablespoons sugar
3 tablespoons flour
2 tablespoons vinegar**

Sprinkle ribs with salt and pepper and brown well in oil in Dutch oven. Add one of the sliced onions and the water. Cover and simmer 2 to 3 hours or until meat is tender. Add additional water if needed. Transfer ribs to platter. In Dutch oven, add enough water to make two cups of liquid, remove and set aside. Return three tablespoons liquid to Dutch oven. Add sugar to liquid and cook for 1 minute. Add remaining two sliced onions and continue cooking and stirring until onions are tender. Blend in flour. Stir in reserved pan juices and cook until thickened. Return ribs to gravy until heated through; serve ribs and gravy with rice. Serves 4 to 6.

SPECIALTY DISHES

••

NO FUSS RIBS

3 1/2 pounds venison ribs, trim excess fat,
  cut in serving size pieces
1/4 cup flour
1 onion, chopped
1 green pepper, chopped
1 clove garlic, minced
1 1/2 cups barbecue sauce

Shake flour in large size (14" x 20") Reynolds Oven Cooking Bag; place in large baking pan. Mix onion, green pepper, garlic and barbecue sauce in cooking bag. Squeeze bag to blend ingredients. Place ribs in bag; turn bag to coat ribs with sauce. Arrange bag in baking pan so that ribs form an even layer. Close bag with nylon tie; make several small slits in top of bag. Bake in preheated oven at 325°F for 1-1/2 to 2 hours, or until meat is tender.

SPECIALTY DISHES

•••

PLEASE PASS THOSE VENISON RIBS (AND HURRY!)

4 pounds venison ribs
1/3 cup soy sauce
1/2 cup pink Chablis
1/2 teaspoon garlic salt
3 1/2 tablespoons brown sugar
1/2 cup water

Place ribs in large roasting pan. Combine remaining ingredients and pour over ribs. Cover. Bake 45 minutes in 350°F oven, turning ribs several times. Remove lid and continue cooking until golden brown and well done (turning periodically). Add more water to sauce if necessary to keep ribs from sticking. Baste with sauce periodically throughout entire cooking time. Serves 4 to 5.

Busy-Day Recipes

••

Given the pressures of our modern lifestyles, we often don't have the time we'd like to cook an evening meal. The following recipes were selected because you can easily prepare a satisfying dinner in a short period of time with a minimum of effort.

With our hectic schedule these days, we often can't spend a great deal of time in the kitchen. These recipes, such as the Venison & Potato Skillet Supper pictured here (see page 194), are some of my favorites when time is precious and I want a quick, easy, and delicious meal.

Busy-Day Recipes

◆◆◆

Recipes

Busy-Day Recipes

◆◆

George's Favorite - Elk Egg Rolls

   2 pounds ground elk
   1 medium onion, chopped
   2 tablespoons cooking oil
   12 Egg roll skins
   Longhorn cheese, cut in 12 strips 1/4" x 3"
   3/4 to 1 cup green chili

Brown ground elk with onion in small amount of oil. Fill each egg roll skin with meat and onion mixture, a strip of longhorn cheese and green chili to taste. Roll up egg rolls and seal edges, moisten with water to seal. Brown stuffed egg rolls in oil until golden brown. Serve with salsa.

This recipe compliments of George & Jean Taulman, U.S. Outfitters, Inc., Taos, New Mexico

Venison & Potato Skillet Supper

   2 pounds ground venison
   2 tablespoons cooking oil
   1/2 cup onion, diced
   1/2 teaspoon salt
   1/4 teaspoon celery salt
   1/8 teaspoon pepper
   3 cups potatoes, grated
   1 tablespoon powdered instant chicken bouillon
   1 cup water
   3 tablespoons dry bread crumbs
   4 to 5 tablespoons grated cheddar cheese

In a large skillet, cook onions in oil until translucent. Add venison, salts and pepper, and cook until meat loses its pink color and begins to brown. Add potatoes and cook 5 minutes longer. Add bouillon and water and simmer 20 to 30 minutes until potatoes are tender. Sprinkle with bread crumbs and cheese just before serving. Serves 6.

Busy-Day Recipes

••

Strip Steak & Onions

    1 pound venison steak
    1/2 teaspoon meat tenderizer
    1/2 teaspoon leaf oregano
    2 tablespoons cornstarch
    1 teaspoon parsley flakes
    3 tablespoons sherry
    1/2 teaspoon salt
    4 large onions, sliced
    2 tablespoons cooking oil

Cut meat into strips 1/4 inch wide and 3 to 5 inches long. Place strips in a bowl. Add meat tenderizer, oregano, cornstarch, parsley and sherry. Sprinkle with salt. Mix and let stand at least 15 minutes. Separate onion slices into rings and fry in oil in a heavy skillet for 2 to 4 minutes, stirring constantly. They should still be somewhat crisp. Remove to a heated platter. Place steak strips into a skillet, stirring constantly for 2 to 4 minutes longer. Add more oil if needed. Put onions back into the skillet and heat through with meat. Serve at once. Serves 4.

Steaks With White Wine

    4 venison steaks, each about 1 1/2 inches thick
    Salt
    Pepper
    2 tablespoons butter
    4 tablespoons dry white wine
    4 tablespoons water

Salt and pepper steaks to taste. Brown steaks in butter in heavy skillet, approximately 5 minutes on each side. Add white wine and cover. Simmer 20 to 25 minutes or until completely done. Add more water if necessary. Serves 4.

BUSY-DAY RECIPES

◆◆◆

VENISON IN FOIL

3 tablespoons butter or margarine
1 1/2 to 2 pounds venison steak
1 envelope onion soup mix (1 3/8 ounce)
1 envelope tomato soup mix (1 3/8 ounce)
1/2 teaspoon garlic salt
1/4 teaspoon seasoned salt

Dot butter on pieces of aluminum foil large enough to wrap meat completely. Mix soup mixes and salts in a small bowl. Sprinkle half of mixture on meat, turn meat and sprinkle remaining mixture on the other side. Dot with remaining butter and wrap securely in foil. Cook over open campfire or bake in 350°F oven for 1 hour. (Time would vary somewhat over campfire, depending on the temperature of fire and how close to the coals the meat is placed.) Serves 6.

GRANDMA'S VENISON

6 slices of leftover cooked venison roast, cut 1 inch thick
2 tablespoons olive oil
1/4 to 1/2 teaspoon garlic salt
1/2 teaspoon onion salt
18 ounces canned baked beans
1 cup mild barbecue sauce (your choice)
4 strips bacon, fried crisp and crumbled

Brush oil on both sides of venison. Sprinkle with garlic and onion salt. Grill over coals 8 to 10 minutes until well browned on each side. Meanwhile, heat beans. Turn meat and spread beans carefully on one side of meat. Spoon barbecue sauce over beans. Cook until second side is well browned. Then carefully lift each piece onto warmed plates. Serves 6.

BUSY-DAY RECIPES

◆◆

EASY VENISON ROAST

> **3 pound venison roast**
> **1/2 medium onion, sliced**
> **2 celery stalks, chopped**
> **1/2 cup ketchup**
> **1/3 lemon juice**
> **1/2 teaspoon Worcestershire sauce**
> **1/2 teaspoon A-1 sauce**
> **1/4 teaspoon salt**
> **1/4 teaspoon garlic salt**
> **1/4 teaspoon pepper**

Place roast in electric crock pot or slow cooker. Add all ingredients and simmer 6 to 8 hours or until tender. Serves 6 to 8.

SPICED ROAST STRIPS

> **2 tablespoons margarine**
> **2 tablespoons flour**
> **1 cup light cream**
> **1/4 teaspoon salt**
> **1/8 teaspoon pepper**
> **2 tablespoons tarragon**
> **1/2 teaspoon leaf basil**
> **1 teaspoon brandy**
> **8 slices cooked venison roast, each about 6 X 4 X 1/2 inches**

Melt margarine in a heavy skillet. Stir in flour until mixture is golden brown. Reduce heat to low and stir in cream, mixing constantly until smooth. When mixture comes to a boil and thickens, add salt pepper, tarragon, basil and brandy. Lay venison slices in the sauce and heat through over low heat. Serve with rice. Serves 6 to 8.

BUSY-DAY RECIPES

VENISON PIZZA DELIGHT

1 pound ground venison
1/2 cup quick-cooking oatmeal
1/4 teaspoon parsley flakes
1/4 teaspoon oregano
1/2 teaspoon onion salt
1/4 teaspoon garlic salt
1 1/2 tablespoons salad oil
1 cup Marinara Sauce
1 cup water
1 package refrigerated butterflake dinner rolls (12 rolls)
1 cup ricotta cheese
4 ounces shredded mozzarella cheese
1 1/2 tablespoons Parmesan cheese

Preheat oven to 375°F. Lightly mix venison, oatmeal, parsley flakes, oregano, onion salt and garlic salt. Brown mixture in oil until completely cooked, breaking into small pieces with a fork. Add Marinara Sauce and water. Bring to a boil; reduce heat and simmer 20 minutes or until very thick. Remove dinner rolls from package and separate each roll in half to make 24 thinner rolls. Layer 12 rolls on bottom of 9-inch pie plate. Press edges together to cover bottom. Spoon 1/2-cup ricotta evenly over roll layer. Top with half of cooked meat mixture. Sprinkle with 1/2 cup mozzarella. Repeat layers of ricotta, meat and mozzarella. Top with remaining rolls. Bake in 375°F oven for 15 minutes. Sprinkle with Parmesan cheese; bake 5 minutes more until rolls are golden brown. Cut into wedges. Serves 4 to 6.

BUSY-DAY RECIPES

◆◆

VENISON STROGANOFF

1 medium onion, chopped
2 tablespoons cooking oil
1 1/2 pounds venison, cut in strips 1/2" wide, 1/4" thick, 2" long
10 3/4 ounce can condensed tomato soup
4 ounce can chopped mushrooms
3/4 teaspoon sugar
1 cup sour cream

In large skillet, sauté onion in oil until translucent. Add venison strips and cook until meat is barely pink inside. Stir in tomato soup, mushrooms, mushroom liquid and sugar. Cover and simmer 30 minutes. Stir in sour cream and heat just to boiling point (do not boil). Serve over hot buttered noodles or rice. Serves 4 to 6.

VENISON TAMALE PIE

1 pound ground venison
1/2 teaspoon salt
1/4 teaspoon pepper
1/4 cup onion, shredded
1/4 teaspoon garlic powder
2 teaspoons chili powder
15 ounces creamed corn (2 cups)
2 cups whole tomatoes, undrained
1/2 cup sliced black olives
2 ounces canned green chilies, diced
1/3 cup corn meal

Sprinkle meat with salt and pepper, and brown with onions. Add garlic powder, chili powder, corn, tomatoes, olives and green chilies. Mix in cornmeal; continue stirring until mixture boils. Simmer 20 to 30 minutes. Serves 4.

BUSY-DAY RECIPES

◆◆◆

VENISON FLAUTAS

2 cups thinly sliced strips of leftover venison roast
1 tablespoon cooking oil
1 tablespoon red wine vinegar
1 1/2 teaspoon chili powder
1/2 teaspoon salt
1/2 teaspoon crumbled leaf oregano
1/2 clove garlic, minced finely
Cooking oil
12 corn tortillas
Salsa

In skillet, brown meat in hot oil. Drain. Add vinegar, chili powder, salt, oregano and garlic. Toss to coat. Set aside. Pour oil to a depth of 1 inch in saucepan. Heat. Fry each tortilla briefly on each side just until soft but not browned (about 5 seconds). Drain tortillas on paper toweling. Spoon meat into tortillas. Roll up and secure with toothpicks. Fry in hot oil in saucepan until crisp (about 2 minutes). Remove carefully from saucepan and top with salsa. Serves 6.

Busy-Day Recipes

◆◆◆

Rio Grande Casserole

1 to 1 1/2 pounds ground venison
1/2 cup chopped green peppers
1 medium onion, chopped
1/4 teaspoon garlic salt
4 ounces canned green chilies
2 cups cottage cheese
4 ounces ripe olives
8 ounces canned green chili salsa (sauce)
1/2 cup grated cheddar cheese
1/2 cup grated Monterey jack cheese
10-ounce package tortilla chips
3/4 cup guacamole
1/2 cup sour cream
1 tomato, diced

Brown meat with peppers, onion, garlic salt and chilies. In a greased baking dish, layer cottage cheese, olives and green chili salsa. Mix cheeses and chips together, add to baking dish and top with the meat mixture. Bake at 350°F for 20 to 30 minutes. Serve topped with guacamole, sour cream and diced tomatoes. Serves 4 to 6.

Busy-Day Recipes

◆◆

Venison Tacos

    1 tablespoon cooking oil
    1 1/2 pounds ground venison
    1/4 teaspoon garlic salt
    1 teaspoon instant chopped onion
    1/8 teaspoon basil
    1/2 teaspoon salt
    1/4 cup tomato sauce
    2 tablespoons salsa sauce
    1 dozen crisp pre-formed taco shells
    1 1/2 cup grated cheddar cheese
    1 cup chopped lettuce
    1/2 cup onion, diced
    2 tomatoes, diced
    3/4 cup bottled taco sauce

Heat oil in skillet. Brown venison in skillet with garlic salt, onion, basil and salt. Add tomato and salsa sauces and heat through. Fill taco shells with a small amount of meat mixture, cheese, onion, lettuce, tomatoes and top with taco sauce. Serves 4 to 6.

Busy-Day Recipes

Venison Tostadas

1 pound ground venison
1 tablespoon cooking oil
1/2 cup chopped onion
1 clove garlic, minced
1/2 teaspoon chili powder
1/2 teaspoon salt
Cooking oil
6 to 10 small flour tortillas
8 ounces canned refried beans (1 cup)
3 large tomatoes, chopped
2 cups shredded lettuce
1 1/2 cups grated cheddar cheese
1 cup salsa sauce

In skillet, brown meat in oil with onion and garlic until meat is brown and onion is tender. Add chili powder and salt. In another skillet fry tortillas in hot oil approximately 30 seconds on each side, or until crisp. Drain excess oil on paper towel. Heat refried beans in a small saucepan. Assemble tostadas by placing a tortilla on a plate and layering meat, beans, tomato, lettuce and cheese on top of the tortilla. Top with salsa sauce. Serve at once. Makes 6 to 10 tostadas.

Busy-Day Recipes

◆◆◆

Venison Chili Salad

1 head iceberg lettuce
2 cups corn chips
2 tomatoes, diced
1 green pepper, diced
1 cup shredded cheddar cheese
15 ounces ripe black olives, drained
2 cups venison chili (use your favorite recipe from this book!)

Cut lettuce into chunks in salad bowl. Add tomatoes, green pepper, cheese, olives and chips. Warm chili and toss with salad. Serve warm.

Louisiana Burgers

1 1/2 pounds ground venison
1 cup cooked rice
3 drops red hot sauce
3 tablespoons tomato sauce
Pinch of sugar
1/2 teaspoon salt
1/4 teaspoon pepper
4 hamburger buns
1 small green pepper, sliced into rings

Mix venison, rice, hot sauce, tomato sauce, sugar, salt and pepper in a bowl. Make 4 patties. Grill over coals until done. Place on buns and top with green pepper rings. Serves 4.

Busy-Day Recipes

◆◆

Venison Patties

2 pounds ground venison
1/2 cup dry bread crumbs
1/4 teaspoon marjoram
1/8 teaspoon nutmeg
1/4 teaspoon pepper
1/2 teaspoon salt
2 tablespoons onion, minced
1 clove garlic, minced
1 egg
2 to 4 tablespoons melted butter

In a medium-sized bowl mix all ingredients except for the butter. Form mixture into 8 patties. Brush with melted butter and broil in oven or over outdoor coals. Turn once. Brush with butter again

Imperial Venison Burgers

1 pound ground venison
Salt
Pepper
Garlic salt
4 tablespoons melted butter or margarine
3 medium potatoes, sliced
2 small onions, sliced
3 carrots, sliced

Form meat into 4 patties. Sprinkle with salt, pepper and garlic salt. Place patties on large pieces of buttered aluminum foil. Layer potatoes, onions and carrots on top of each patty. Salt and pepper vegetables. Drizzle remaining butter over everything. Seal each packet. Grill over open coals about 20 minutes on each side or until everything is well done.

Busy-Day Recipes

◆◆◆

Salisbury Patties

1 pound ground venison
1 package dry onion soup mix
1/4 cup bread or cracker crumbs
1 egg
2 tablespoons oil
2 tablespoons flour
1 1/2 cups water
1 can mushrooms, drained

Use a fork and lightly combine meat, one-half onion soup mix, crumbs, milk and egg. Shape into patties and brown in skillet in oil. Pour off most of the fat. Add remaining soup mix and flour. Gradually stir in water and mushrooms. Cover and cook over low heat for 20 to 30 minutes, stirring occasionally.

This recipe compliments of Bruce & Elaine Koffler, Koffler Boats, Junction City, Oregon

BUSY-DAY RECIPES

••

ITALIAN STYLE DEERBURGERS

1 1/2 pounds ground venison
2 teaspoons parsley
1 clove garlic, minced
1/2 teaspoon leaf oregano
1/2 teaspoon basil
3/4 teaspoon salt
1/8 teaspoon pepper
2 tablespoons grated onion
2 tablespoons grated Parmesan cheese
4 thin slices mozzarella cheese
4 wedges Italian bread, toasted and buttered

Mix meat with parsley, garlic, oregano, basil, salt, pepper, onion and Parmesan cheese. Shape into 4 patties. Grill over coals. When meat is cooked through, top each burger with mozzarella cheese and melt. Place on buttered, toasted Italian bread. Serves 4.

STUFFED BURGERS

1 1/2 pounds ground venison
3 tablespoons onion, grated
2 garlic cloves, minced
2 teaspoons parsley flakes
1/2 teaspoon salt
3/4 cup cheddar cheese, grated
4 thin slices of large onion

Mix venison, onion, garlic, parsley and salt. Form into 8 thin patties. Place cheese and onion slice on four of the patties. Place a second patty on the top and press edges to seal. Grill outdoors over coals. Sprinkle with salt as they cook. Cook until well done. Serves 4.

BUSY-DAY RECIPES

••

ITALIAN MEATLOAF SANDWICHES

Leftover meatloaf
1 loaf Italian bread
1/2 cup butter
1/2 teaspoon dried leaf oregano
1/2 teaspoon leaf basil
2 tablespoons Parmesan cheese

Preheat oven to 350°F. Cut bread loaf into 1/2 inch slices, keeping them in order. Cut meatloaf into slices approximately the same shape as bread slices. In a small saucepan melt the butter with the oregano, basil and cheese. Brush butter mixture on both sides of meat and bread. Make a new loaf on a large sheet of aluminum foil by adding a slice of meatloaf between each slice of bread. Wrap securely in aluminum foil and heat in oven for 20 to 30 minutes or until heated through. Serves 4 - 6.

JERKY & SAUSAGE

Jerky is one of the oldest methods of meat curing. All early man had to do was to immerse meat strips in ocean water, dry it in the sun, and a quick supply of meat was ensured. Today we still brine meat in a salt water solution, but we mix in other flavorings to spice it up a bit.

This is one curing process that allows you to use all your imagination and creativity. With salt as the basis, you can add all sorts of spices — the list is endless. Happily, the end product is a piece of meat that quickly suffices as a snack while you're hunting, fishing, hiking, or just driving down the road.

If you've ever purchased a stick of beef jerky at a gas station or convenience store, you know how outrageous the cost is. Venison jerky is just as good, and infinitely cheaper to make at home. What's more, the jerking process will neutralize every hint of gaminess in the nastiest cuts of meat.

A couple of tips: When cutting strips of meat, always slice against the grain. To ensure uniformly thick slices of meat, cut frozen meat just as it's starting to thaw. It will be firm and much more easily sliced.

The easiest way to make jerky is to lay the seasoned meat (it should be allowed to soak in the flavored brine in a refrigerator for several hours — see individual recipes) in cookie sheets that are covered with aluminum foil. Place the meat on the foil so the pieces don't touch; when the sheet is full, put in an oven pre-heated to 180 degrees. Close the door and bake for one hour; then remove the sheet from the oven. At this point the meat should be thoroughly moist with plenty of juice in the cookie sheet. Carefully carry the sheet to the sink or disposal container and gently tip up the sheet to allow as much juice as possible to flow out. Then turn over the meat slices, and put them back in the oven which has now been turned down to 140 degrees which is normally the lowest setting. Open the oven door a bit to allow moisture to escape. Remember, the object here is to quick-dry the meat, NOT to bake, cook, or roast it. Keep checking the jerky every half hour or so, and turn it as required. My method of determining its doneness is to hold a sample by each end and bend it. If it acts like rubber, it isn't done; if it "snaps with a clean break;" it's ready.

If you have several cookie sheets, lay them on top of each other, but try to lay them so they don't entirely cover each other. Leave room for moisture to escape. You'll note that the meat in the sheet on the bottom rack, which is closest to the heat coils, will dry fastest. Rotate the cookie sheets around for uniform drying.

All in all the process should take four to six hours. For the best results, keep checking and turning the meat. If you leave it on its own too long, it won't be ruined, but will be extremely hard and brittle, losing much of the flavor. Fuss over your jerky as you dry it, and you'll have a much better product.

Jerky & Sausage

◆◆

Sausage is nothing more than seasoned ground meat that's mixed with seasonings, stuffed in casings, cooked or smoked, and refrigerated until used. Some sausages require pork meat or pork or beef suet to be added, and some sausages aren't stuffed in casings at all, but are simply fried or grilled as patties.

Many folks are afraid to try sausage making because they perceive it to be too complicated. It's really an easy process. Once you've tried it, you'll wonder why it took you so long, especially since sausage is expensive to buy. Most meat processors will take in your venison on a trade and make it into sausage, or will trade you for sausage already made up. State laws don't allow you to buy venison, but you can "trade" your own. That seems like a good deal, but there's a catch. The processor charges you for his time and spices. When you write the check, expect to pay at least one dollar a pound for your own meat that someone else made sausage out of. If that sounds unnecessary and expensive, you're right. Make the sausage yourself.

As a tip, health experts say that sausage will be safe if cooked for one hour at 150 degrees before being stored for later use. This process will kill the normal bacteria found in pork and uncooked meat. Be sure, however, to keep the meat chilled as you normally would before and after you bake or smoke it.

Recipes

JERKY & SAUSAGE

••

E-Z JERKY

Venison in any whole form
Seasoned salt
Coarse Black Pepper
Liquid smoke

Slice venison across the grain as thinly as possible. Coat all pieces thoroughly with seasoned salt and pepper and brush lightly with liquid smoke. Drape slices of meat on oven racks so all sides are exposed to the air. Set oven at 175°F and cook for one hour, then reduce heat to 140°F and continue drying, with oven door ajar, for 6 to 7 hours. Turn meat over every hour or so for even drying.

AIR-DRIED VENISON

3 pounds venison, cut into strips 6" x 2" x 1"
2 pounds salt
4 tablespoons allspice
5 tablespoons pepper

Mix salt, allspice and pepper and rub this curing mixture on meat thoroughly. Tie meat strips with string and hang inside a wire-mesh box to keep insects away. Hang box in a sunny spot and let meat dry in fresh air for about two weeks to one month, until desired dryness occurs. Never let the meat get wet during the drying period. As a variation, dry meat in a smoker.

••

VENISON SUMMER SAUSAGE

4 pounds pork
12 pounds venison
3 tablespoons meat tenderizer
1/2 cup smoke salt
3 teaspoons pepper
1 teaspoon liquid smoke
3 tablespoons whole mustard seed

Grind pork and venison together in meat grinder. Add remaining ingredients and mix well. Cover with plastic wrap and let stand overnight in a cool place. Stuff into sausage casings. Tie shut and let stand in cool place overnight. Smoke for about four hours and leave sausage in smoker overnight. Then smoke another four hours, and then put in a pre-heated oven and cook for one hour at 150°F. Keep refrigerated until served.

MINT SAUSAGE PATTIES

1 3/4 pounds ground venison
1 3/4 pounds ground pork
1 tablespoon salt
1 teaspoon red cayenne pepper
1/8 teaspoon garlic powder
1 teaspoon cumin
1 teaspoon poultry seasoning
1/8 teaspoon sage
1/8 teaspoon curry powder
1 teaspoon dried mint, or 5 leaves fresh mint, diced

Grind the venison and pork together and mix well. Then mix in the rest of the ingredients. Form into patties and fry until browned and cooked through.

JERKY & SAUSAGE

••

RIO GRANDE SALAMI

4 pounds ground venison
1/2 pound ground beef suet
2 teaspoons black pepper
1/2 teaspoon onion salt
1 1/2 teaspoons garlic powder
5 teaspoons salt
2 1/2 teaspoons liquid smoke
1 1/2 teaspoons small red chilies

Mix all ingredients in a non-metal bowl. Refrigerate for 3 days, thoroughly mixing each day with hands. On the fourth day divide mixture into 5 parts. Knead and form into long thin logs, about 12 inches long. Place logs on cookie sheet and bake at 155°F. After 5 hours, turn logs over and cook 5 hours more. Remove from oven and roll in paper towels to remove excess grease. Cool, wrap in foil and keep in refrigerator. Makes five, 12-inch logs.

RIGHT-NOW SAUSAGE

2 pounds ground venison
1 teaspoon garlic salt
1/2 teaspoon onion salt
1 tablespoon liquid smoke
2 tablespoons sesame seeds
3 tablespoons curing salt

Place all ingredients in a bowl and mix well. Roll into a log shape, wrap in aluminum foil, and bake in a pre-heated oven at 350°F for 1 to 1-1/2 hours.

JERKY & SAUSAGE

GRILLED JERKY

Venison strips
1 gallon water
1/2 pound salt
Sugar
Caraway seed
Curry powder

Cut venison into strips 1 to 1 1/2 inches wide and about 5 inches long. Mix water and salt in a glass or plastic container. Add meat. Weight it so liquid covers the entire surface of it. (A good weight is a heavy glass plate placed on top of meat to sink it down into the liquid.) Brine meat for 24 to 36 hours. Remove the meat and rinse with fresh water. Sprinkle sugar moderately on meat. Place meat on broiler tray. Make a mixture of 1 part caraway seed (browned in oven and ground) to 2 parts curry powder. Sprinkle on meat and broil about 10 inches from heat in oven for 20 to 30 minutes.

Remove meat and smoke in a covered charcoal grill as follows: Place a small pile of charcoal briquettes in one corner of grill and light. Soak hickory chips in water for 30 minutes and then place on charcoal after it is burning well. Arrange chips so they cover charcoal completely. Place venison strips on the far corner of grill. Lower lid and smoke for 2 to 3 hours, keeping top and bottom vents open.

JERKY & SAUSAGE

If you have a smoker, try drying your venison in it rather than in an oven. The meat will have a much more robust flavor.

COMMERCIAL JERKY MIX

After years of fooling with dozens of jerky recipes, I found a commercial seasoning mix that is absolutely wonderful. So good, that I don't mind sharing it in this book. I promise that this jerky mix will transform the gamiest venison into the finest jerky you've ever had.

For information, contact:

HI MOUNTAIN JERKY, INC.
715 E. Roosevelt
PO Box 1821
Riverton, Wyoming 82501
(307) 856-6626

Page 216

Amazing Venison Recipes
INDEX

INDEX

INDEX

INDEX

INDEX

INDEX

ABOUT THE AUTHOR

Jim Zumbo has been cooking ever since he began forestry college in 1958. He incorporated many of his family's Italian recipes in his initial cooking, and then started branching out to a variety of other types of foods. As a college student, most of Jim's menus consisted of wild game simply because he was too broke to buy beef and always seemed to have a deer steak or two in the freezer.

Jim decided early on that he really liked to cook and took pleasure in sharing his kitchen delights with family, friends and neighbors. Throughout his thirty-some years of traveling and hunting both here and abroad, Jim has gathered hundreds of recipes. This book is a compilation of his very favorites from his vast collection.

Jim is Hunting Editor of Outdoor Life magazine and has been with the publication as a full-time editor since 1978. He has written more than 1,000 articles for all the major outdoor magazines, many of them on cooking wild game. This is his 15th book. Jim lives in Cody, Wyoming with his wife Madonna.

OTHER BOOKS & VIDEOS BY JIM ZUMBO

TO HECK WITH ELK HUNTING
Jim's favorite hunting tales. Most are humorous, but some are bizarre. Says Pat McManus, "Zumbo finally tells the naked truth about elk hunting. And about time, too." Illustrated by Boots Reynolds. Hardcover. 186 pages. $17.95

TO HECK WITH DEER HUNTING
Packed with tales of deer hunts around the continent, from Canada to Mexico; New York to Washington. Humorous tales of several dozen hunts, of which about half are whitetails; the others about muleys and blacktails. Hardcover. 188 pages. $17.95

CALLING ALL ELK
The only book on the subject of elk hunting that covers every aspect of elk vocalization. Softcover. 200 pages. $14.95

HUNT ELK
The most comprehensive book ever written on elk hunting. This 260 page hardcover describes everything you've ever wanted to know about elk - bugling, hunting in timber, late season hunting, trophy hunting, solid advice on hunting on your own or with an outfitter, and lots more. $24.95

HUNTING AMERICA'S MULE DEER
The first book ever done on every phase of mule deer hunting. This thick 360-page hardcover is acclaimed to be the best on the subject. Plenty of photos, with valuable information on trophy hunting and where-to, and how-to hunt muley bucks. $19.95

HUNTING BUGLING ELK WITH JIM ZUMBO
Produced by Sportsmen On Film -70 minutes. Watch Jim fly in to Idaho's Selway wilderness and hunt elk. This video is loaded with instructions and tips on elk bugling, and is climaxed by Jim taking a big 6-point bull on camera. $29.95

OTHER BOOKS & VIDEOS BY JIM ZUMBO

LATE SEASON ELK WITH JIM ZUMBO
Produced by Sportsmen On Film - 38 minutes. See huge elk plowing through deep powder snow, and watch a 12-year old boy take a big bull on camera. Lots of tips and techniques included. $29.95

SUCCESSFUL MULE DEER HUNTING
Produced by 3M Corp. - 60 minutes. Acclaimed to be the best mule deer video ever produced. Watch Jim stalk and kill a nice four-point buck. Plenty of info on techniques. Filmed in Wyoming. $29.95

E-Z COW CALL INSTRUCTIONAL AUDIO TAPE CASSETTE
Produced by Jim Zumbo - 30 minutes. Jim Zumbo tells where, how and when to use the E-Z Call, including hunt scenarios and situations. $9.95

E-Z COW CALL
The most versatile, easy-to-use call ever invented. Attracts elk before, during and after the bugling season. Stops spooked elk. Reassures wary elk. Also calls and stops deer, bear and coyotes. Made of very soft pliable plastic and is easy to blow. Both calling edges are of different lengths to allow calls of varying pitches. $9.95

TO ORDER: Send check, money order or VISA/MC. Credit card orders: please include card number and expiration date. Allow 4-6 weeks for delivery. Shipping and handling charges: add $3.00 for the first item and $1.00 for each additional item.

Jim Zumbo
WAPITI VALLEY PUBLISHING CO.
P.O. Box 2390, Cody, Wyoming 82414
(307) 587-5486 FAX (307) 527-4951

All books will be autographed